BEST OF THE BRITCOMS

BEST OF THE BRITCOMS:

From *Fawlty Towers* to *Absolutely Fabulous*

by

Garry Berman

TAYLOR PUBLISHING COMPANY
DALLAS, TEXAS

Designed by Hespenheide Design

Published by Taylor Publishing Company
1550 West Mockingbird Lane
Dallas, Texas 75235
www.taylorpub.com

Library of Congress Cataloging-in-Publication Data:
Berman, Garry.
    Best of the Britcoms: from Fawlty Towers to Absolutely Fabulous /
by Garry Berman.
        p.   cm.
    Filmography: p.
    Includes bibliographical references and index.
    ISBN 0-87833-160-3
    1. Television comedies—Great Britain.   I. Title.
PN1992.8.C66B47   1999   99-35301
791.45′617′0941—dc21   CIP

10 9 8 7 6 5 4
Printed in the United States of America

To Karen,
whose feelings toward this book have evolved
from that of a skeptic, to supporter, to advocate.

And to Britcom fans everywhere.

CONTENTS

The Britcoms covered in this book are listed below in chronological order according to their original air dates in Britain. They have all aired on American television, and most are continually being aired in various markets across the country. The majority is also available on home video.

Part I

"I didn't get where I am today..." Britcoms of the 1970s

Part II

"Listen very carefully, I shall say this only once..." Britcoms of the 1980s

PART III

"I don't believe it!..." Britcoms of the 1990s

PART IV

Short Takes

FOREWORD

If you enjoy watching British television comedy, living here in Britain proves wonderfully convenient. Whenever the muse strikes, I can simply turn on the telly, sit back, and relax, and with a bit of luck, come across either a current favorite or an old gem. Moreover, as someone who has spent a good deal of my career *performing* British television comedy, living in Britain has proven to be even more convenient than you could imagine!

Ah, but then there are those of you British comedy fans who aren't so fortunate. You're stranded in America or elsewhere, and have to make a bit more of an effort to find some of our funniest sitcoms on your own television stations. Luckily, you know they're there, and have been for many years now. This goes to show that we have exported something of value to you since the Beatles. Mind you, we've enjoyed a good number of comedies you've sent to us. I suppose it's been rather like pen pals exchanging amusing letters. But you don't need me to tell you about your own sitcoms. I do, however, know a thing or two about many of the programs included in this book.

I have nothing but pleasant memories of starring in *The Good Life* (or *Good Neighbors,* as you know it). I was one star among four— Felicity Kendal, Penelope Keith, my dear departed friend Paul Eddington, and myself were all of equal ability and enthusiasm. The warmth and humor among our characters on-screen was reflective of how we felt about each other off-screen. Along with our writers and directors, we were like a family. We later went our separate ways to star in other sitcoms, where lightning even managed to strike again for most of us. You've seen Penelope in *To the Manor Born, Executive Stress,* and others. Paul became Britain's top bureaucrat in *Yes, Minister.* Felicity has appeared in several comedy series, as have I.

Our collective work in television is only a slice of the pie. For every show like *The Good Life*, with a quiet suburban setting, there have been wild, irreverent shows like *The Young Ones* and *Red Dwarf.* The best sitcoms offer their own distinct qualities, and if they make us laugh, then they've succeeded in their mission, no matter the route they may take. I've also seen a lot of rubbish on television here, and you can be thankful that it hasn't survived the trip overseas to you. The best of what we've had to offer has, for the most part, made the journey. And the wonderful reaction to British comedy speaks for itself! It's more popular in America now than it's ever been. Just the right time for *Best of the Britcoms.* Here you can learn a few things about your favorite comedies that you didn't know before,

and even discover a few series that you may have missed the first time around.

Whichever your favorites may be, enjoy, and keep laughing.

Richard Briers

ACKNOWLEDGMENTS

Thanks to Jenny Secombe at the BBC, who, way back when I first presented my idea to her, was the first person to say the magic words, "Yes, we'll help you." Thanks also to the following agents in Britain: Vivian Clore, Sheila Lemon, Brian Codd, Peter Froggatt, St. John Donald, Lorna Stacy, and Christian Hodell. Without them, I wouldn't have made much progress in my efforts to contact those who created the successful Britcoms we now enjoy.

Many thanks to the following people who graciously agreed to speak with me about their work: actors Gorden Kaye, Peter Bowles, Richard Briers, and Julia St. John; writers George Layton, David Renwick, Andrew Norriss, Roy Clarke, Eric Chappell, Peter Spence, Michael Aitkens, Peter Tilbury, Maurice Gran, and Paul Mayhew-Archer; director/producers David Croft, Harold Snoad, John Lloyd, Gareth Gwenlan, Susan Belbin, and Ed Bye.

A special thanks to the BBC and its helpful and patient staff, namely Claire Wilson, Siobhan O'Neill, Colin Ross, and Mary Collins. An extra special thank you goes to Eva de Romarate, who, in the early days of my research, was my lifeline to the "Beeb." In her capacity as Assistant Press and Publicity officer, Eva never failed, despite her own busy workload, to try her best to obtain materials, phone numbers, and countless miscellaneous bits of information for me that have proved invaluable to this book. Eva has since moved elsewhere within the BBC, but will forever have my gratitude for her help in making this book possible.

More thank yous go to Yorkshire Television, Jane Foster at Pearson Television, Linda Athayde, Lucy Spencer, Susan Harvie, and David Meyerson for their contributions to my research. The Altair Literary Agency and Nicholas Smith get a special thanks, as do Julius Cain at BBC Worldwide Americas, and Michelle Street.

Of course, I owe a debt of gratitude to my editor, Camille Cline, for her support and good judgment. Thanks also to Fred Francis for helping me with the details.

And, finally, I must express my heartfelt appreciation to my family and friends for their encouragement, support, and patience.

PREFACE

The idea for this book was born during an unexpected brainstorm at my favorite local diner. I suddenly decided over a cheeseburger deluxe that I should do something constructive with my personal video library of over 200 hours of Britcoms on nearly 100 tapes (a collection that continues to grow almost exponentially). Why not share my passion for British television comedy with other American fans who have long enjoyed these shows, but have not had an opportunity to learn much about them? And so the labor of love began, and the first phone call was made.

This book is not intended to be all-inclusive. The programs celebrated here are not necessarily the *only* British comedies worth seeking out and enjoying, and the exclusion of others is not meant to imply that they aren't well made or funny enough to be worth

our viewing time. After careful deliberation we have here the cream of the crop, reaching back a quarter of a century. The section for each program contains synopses of individual episodes, many of which can be considered the "best" (a subjective matter, obviously), but more importantly are meant to be representative of that series as a whole.

Also, there have been several successful British comedy programs seen in the U.S. that can't be labeled as situation comedies in the conventional sense such as *Ripping Yarns* and *The Darling Buds of May*. Then there are the sketch programs and panel shows such as *Alas Smith and Jones, French and Saunders, Alexei Sayle's Stuff, Mr. Bean*, and *Whose Line Is It, Anyway?*, which, while they are not examined in detail, are mentioned in passing from time to time throughout these pages.

INTRODUCTION:
THE CASE FOR THE BRITCOM

Whenever I have the opportunity to gingerly steer a conversation to one of my favorite topics, i.e., British sitcoms, the exchange often proceeds thusly:

Me: "Yes, I've been a big fan of British sitcoms for many years."

Them: "Oh, you mean like Benny Hill?"

Well, not exactly.

Don't get me wrong. The late Benny Hill is considered a true comic genius (if rarely a politically correct one) who wrote all of his sketches, songs, and monologues himself. But no, his shows were not sitcoms. *Monty Python's Flying Circus*, for that matter, wasn't a sitcom either. It was arguably the most brilliant comedy program of all time on either side of the Atlantic, but it was most definitely not a sitcom.

All Americans know what a sitcom is—a half-hour comedy with a storyline of some sort (maybe two), most often with a beginning, middle, and end by the time the half-hour is over. In contrast, Britain's comedy writers, directors, and performers have often created programs that defy neat categorization. The sitcom rules are often challenged, rewritten, or thrown out. Boundaries are tested and pushed, and the sitcom form itself is sometimes stretched in innovative ways almost unknown to American audiences. Of course, not every Britcom makes this claim. Many are as conventional as the majority of American sitcoms. As a whole though, they are highly creative examples of television comedy at its best. Viewers in Britain are lucky to have such easy access to them, but Americans can enjoy them too. Public television stations in most major television markets across the country include Britcoms on their schedules. In addition, more than half of the series featured in this book are available for sale on home video.

In the early 1970s, Britcoms made a tentative appearance on American airwaves in some cities with programs such as *Doctor in the House* and *Father Dear Father*, both popular programs in Britain, but little more than short-lived novelties here. It wasn't until *Monty Python's Flying Circus* opened the British comedy floodgates in the U.S. in 1974 that viewers became aware of what British television had to offer. The runaway popularity of *Python* was due mostly to word-of-mouth by those who had stumbled upon it while switching channels (before we called it "surfing") on Sunday nights. It didn't take long for this bizarre, relentlessly funny, and sometimes mind-bending show to become a legend.

Monty Python is a story unto itself, but it can be largely credited for the great anticipation and subsequent popularity of *Fawlty Towers*. John Cleese's built-in recognition factor and wonderfully manic performance didn't hurt either.

This one-two punch served as the beginning of the Britcom "invasion." Public television stations, delighted by the success of these two shows, quickly became hungry for more. Discriminating fans took the trouble to seek out new Britcoms on TV stations that they might have otherwise neglected. In the past ten years alone, over sixty comedy series from Britain have appeared on American TV at one time or another, mostly on PBS stations but also on national cable networks such as A&E and Comedy Central (the new BBC America cable channel provides yet another outlet for Britcoms). Such exposure to the best of these Britcoms has enabled us to compare and contrast the ways in which British and American sitcoms are created.

First of all, there are basic structural differences between American and British television. The brutal truth is that American networks are businesses. They have to please advertisers who want good ratings for the programs on which they buy time for their commercials. A consequence of this, however, is that new shows with modest ratings are usually not given much time to find their audience or to work out creative kinks. Britain has commercial television as well, where ratings can determine the lifespan of any given series. However, on the non-commercial BBC channels, where audience numbers are also measured, a rating called "Audience Appreciation" comes into play. A program with a relatively small audience but with high AA numbers is given time to stake a claim. Several of the series discussed in this book got off to slow and uncertain starts (referred to as "slow burners"), only to grow in popularity over time.

The differences in the creative process between the two countries begin at the beginning, with the script. British writers are quick to point out that they most often write either alone or in teams of two, and those who create a sitcom usually remain with it for the duration of its run. For instance, Roy Clarke created the series *Open All Hours* and wrote each episode himself. The same is true for most other sitcom writers and their respective creations, whether they write alone or with a partner. Many times, when writers feel they've exhausted the possibilities of the series in question, they simply pack it in. John Cleese felt that twelve episodes of *Fawlty Towers* was enough. Jennifer Saunders knew that the third series of *Absolutely Fabulous* would be the last, making a grand total of eighteen episodes (compare this with the average number of twenty-two

The prolific Roy Clarke created the series *Open All Hours* and wrote every episode. Here, Granville (David Jason) turns to Nurse Gladys (Lynda Baron) to escape the pestering of his uncle Arkwright (Ronnie Barker). *BBC Worldwide*

episodes for a single season of an American sitcom). Carla Lane, creator and writer of the hit *Butterflies*, also knew to end that series after twenty-seven highly successful episodes rather than run it into the ground. By contrast, an American sitcom that ends its run voluntarily while still in its prime (*The Mary Tyler Moore Show, Cheers, Seinfeld*) actually makes news for doing so. Others remain on the air long after they've outstayed their welcome and have run out of worthwhile ideas.

As for the American sitcom staff writers, the majority of them learn not to get too comfortable in their comfy chairs. Except for the seasoned veterans, they are largely considered expendable. As Rod Taylor points out in the introduction to the invaluable British publication *The Guinness Book of Sitcoms*, "The American networks buy by the metre and vast teams of writers are hired and fired in the quest to deliver hundreds of shows. The mortality rate of writers on *Roseanne* is frightening. At least we in Britain nurse and nurture our writers because without them, there is no beginning."

Peter Spence, creator/writer of the immensely popular *To the Manor Born* (1979–81), has written on his own and "by committee." While he's supportive of the committee system, he believes it has another creative drawback. "...*One Foot in the Grave* or *Reginald Perrin* I don't think you could get out of a committee system, because they are [written with] very individual styles," he said. "You could get all the benefits of the team, but you don't get the individuality of style that runs right through a series. I think that's very difficult to get out of a committee."

In an eloquent essay for the London *Sunday Times*, writer/comedian Julian Dutton agreed. "*Rising Damp* ran for four seasons and was written by one man, Eric Chappell. If one person can write a masterpiece in the sitcom genre (David Renwick and *One Foot in the Grave* are more recent examples) then there can't be that much wrong with our system," Dutton wrote.

As far as sitcom dialogue itself is concerned, it's become a truism that Americans love one-liners. Their favorite dialogue is that which doesn't make them wait too long to laugh. It's been said that Hollywood comedy writers are often ordered to include three jokes per page in the average sitcom script.

As for the British, it's generally accepted that they prefer dialogue in which the comic lines are based more on the characters who are speaking them and the situations in which they find themselves. Hence, it is difficult to pick out one or two random lines from most Britcoms (believe me, I've tried), because they are so enmeshed within the context of the story. Susan Belbin, director of *'Allo, 'Allo!* and *One Foot in the Grave*, said, "In America [the writers] are very much kind of one-line lads...whereas here we're very much kind of character lads and attitude lads. Our comedy comes from the attitudes and characters, and the situations they find themselves in rather than the one-liners...*The Cosby Show* was a great favorite of mine. It had a very human touch. But they're just very, very different."

There is another, more technical aspect of a typical Britcom production that is rarely found in American sitcoms: Most Britcoms have the means to expand beyond the studio walls and film or tape part of each episode on location. A story can bring its characters outdoors for a breath of fresh air, or on location miles away to the countryside or quiet village. It makes perfect sense, and allows for almost infinite storyline possibilities. American sitcoms rarely venture outdoors, usually opting to simulate a location on the indoor set. Even the now-classic *Seinfeld* confined most of its outdoor scenes to a bogus New York sidestreet on the studio backlot.

Veteran Britcom producer Harold Snoad feels that American sitcoms are losing out by resisting location shoots: "Our series are a bit more expansive in as much as we do have location stuff. You have very little; it's always stuck in a studio with you. If you take *The Golden Girls*, even when they had a transition between two scenes, it was a still [photo] of the exterior. They seem to be loath to go out on location and do anything that took them outside."

To be fair, budget and time constraints for a typical American sitcom can have a big influence on production values, such as the use of location shoots. Many Britcoms, however, have demonstrated great imagination with their varied settings.

Seemingly endless comic possibilities and storylines abound when there are no limits on where or when a series can take place. For instance, producer David Croft has created his best series by reexploring earlier periods of his life and finding the comedy potential in a variety of settings. The results can be found in *Dad's Army*, *'Allo, 'Allo!* (both set during World War II) and *Hi-De-Hi* (set at a resort in 1959). And of course *The Black Adder*

Aboard Red Dwarf, hologram Rimmer (Chris Barrie) and surviving crew member Lister (Craig Charles) exchange views. *BBC Worldwide*

series, co-created by and starring Rowan Atkinson, leaps back to the Middle Ages in its first series, and gradually makes its way forward in time and into the twentieth century by the fourth series.

Red Dwarf takes place three million years in the future and uses the entire galaxy as its venue. Our heroes in this sci-fi comedy wander throughout space on their spaceship, and their occasional reappearances on Earth become surreal adventures. *Red Dwarf*'s great success is due in part to its taking full advantage of the possibilities afforded by its setting. At the very least, it's *different*.

By contrast, American sitcoms seem to all take place in the here and now. And they suffer for it to some degree because their creators seem almost oblivious to this inherent limitation. Still, just as American audiences love one-liners, we also love contemporary comedy. *Friends* thrives on its ability to work contemporary popular culture references into its dialogue and stories. *Seinfeld* did the same. But while armchair TV critics have been known to welcome and even praise period dramas on television and film, American situation comedies seem doomed to exist forever in the present (more on this in *The Black Adder* chapter).

Lest all of this sounds a bit like bashing American sitcoms while canonizing their British counterparts, it's only fair to include a few words of praise for American shows by a British writer. As is the case with many British comedy writers, Andrew Norriss, co-creator and writer of *The Brittas Empire*, thoroughly enjoys what our sitcom factories in Hollywood have to offer:

Mind you, I'm quite a fan of American sitcoms. They're the best in the world, I

Absolutely Fabulous became a stateside hit on the cable network Comedy Central. (*Left to right*): Eddy (Jennifer Saunders), Saffy (Julia Sawalha), Bubble (Jane Horrocks), and Patsy (Joanna Lumley). *BBC Worldwide*

think. There's always more warmth in an American sitcom. They always want you to go away feeling good somehow about life. They never let it go really black: *Friends* at the moment, *Cheers* at its height, *Roseanne* at its height—touching stuff I couldn't believe. And the whole use of language and plotting in all of those. I don't think you could find anything better in the world. We all watch it over here.

Harold Snoad said, "The thing I think about it is everyone here says, 'Oh, wonderful American comedies,' and I don't doubt that for a moment, but I think, if we're being very honest, that we see the best over here—probably like you see the best of ours."

But even if Americans really only get to see the very best of British sitcoms, there's no denying that the best of them are very good indeed.

A note about the term "series"

As is often the case when dealing with two or more ways of speaking the same language, the British and Americans are known to give slightly different meanings to some words. Here in the U.S., a television "series" refers to the program itself. *Seinfeld* is a series, that's obvious enough. The same applies to

British television. *Absolutely Fabulous* is a series. That's easy. So where's the confusion?

In British television, sitcoms produce their episodes in batches of six or seven at a time. Each batch is also referred to as a "series." For instance, *Fawlty Towers* ran for two series, one comprising six episodes in 1975, and a second series of six episodes in 1979. American TV viewers are more familiar with the term "season," which traditionally begins each autumn and runs through late spring, consisting of as many as twenty-two episodes per program.

This book has adapted the dual usage of the term "series." The purpose is not to confuse the reader, but to maintain some consistency. Most of the people interviewed throughout the following pages use the word "series" for both its meanings, but the context in which it is used should keep things fairly clear.

Producer Harold Snoad explained why British sitcoms produce such a limited number of episodes at a time. He said, "It's not quite the same now, funnily enough, but in the earlier days, you'd do a series of six or seven then you followed it by a series of six or seven, whichever you haven't done before, the idea being that it made a package of thirteen. Thirteen weeks to a quarter, and most countries wanted to have these sold overseas. Overseas sales to America, Australia, New Zealand, and various other places ran these as [a package of] thirteen. We didn't really want to do thirteen straightaway over here, because if we're doing a new series, we didn't want to put the money into thirteen of them without finding out whether the public over here liked them first. So we used to do either six or seven, and with success we'd do another six or seven, whichever it was that made up the thirteen. It's a nice round figure for overseas sales. Nowadays there are not so many hard and fast rules. It's still a bit six-and-seven, but I've done *Keeping up Appearances* as two lots of ten—it's not quite the same as it was."

From the perspective of the British audience, though, this means they have to wait several months between series. Snoad explained, "What normally happens in this country is that you'll get a series of something every year. Normally the peak time these go out is what we call the autumn schedule. There's one series every year of [a program], so that will go out between September and perhaps February, then that series will be repeated during the summer months."

A Thumbnail History of British Television

Before we take a closer look at the finest Britcoms ever to grace American airwaves, it may be helpful to place them in a historical context, and trace how British television has evolved over the past six decades.

Did you know that the BBC was broadcasting television programs on a regular basis by 1936, more than a decade before American TV networks had gotten their act together?

While no one person invented television, Scotsman John Logie Baird began his first experiments with transmitting sound and pictures as early as 1924. His early work excited both the press and many influential backers, but the BBC hesitated before jumping on the bandwagon. Finally, in 1929, BBC Director-General Sir John Reith gave Baird permission to use BBC transmitters for his demonstrations to BBC engineers. By 1932, after several months of making experimental transmissions, the BBC set up its own television studios, buying much of its equipment from the Baird group. Other countries were also on the way to developing their own television systems (it is interesting to note a scene in the 1933 comedy *International House* with W. C. Fields, in which television, called "radioscope" is demonstrated to a group of wealthy bidders).

By 1936, Baird's chief rival company, Marconi EMI, had been alternating weekly with Baird's system on BBC transmissions. But Marconi EMI had surpassed Baird's technology and ultimately won favor with the BBC. By 1939, about 11,000 TV sets were in use. In September the Nazis invaded Poland, Britain declared war, and all television operations were ordered to shut down.

The BBC reopened its TV service after the war in June of 1946. It was to be the only television service available to Britain until 1954, when the conservative government's bill advocating the establishment of commercial television (to be overseen by the Independent Television Authority) became hotly debated. The bill finally became law in July of 1954, and the Independent Television service began transmitting in September of 1955. Among the fifteen ITV regional production/transmission companies were Associated Rediffusion (for the London area on weekdays), ATV (for London on weekends), Granada TV (northwest England on weekdays), and others, such as services for Scotland and Wales.

It wasn't until April of 1964 that the BBC-2 channel was launched with a production of *Kiss Me Kate*. Shortly thereafter, plans began in earnest to produce color transmissions on a regular basis, but a decision still had to be made regarding a common color transmission system to be used throughout Europe. The BBC had been experimenting between the American NTSC system, the French Secam system, and the German PAL system. The PAL color system prevailed, which enabled the BBC channels and ITV to use a 625-line system rather than 405 lines (translation: a clearer picture with higher resolution). Color on the BBC channels was launched officially in December of 1967 in time for the Beatles' special *Magical Mystery Tour*.

The following year saw still more changes and additions to Britain's television structure. The ITA created three major independent television companies in the summer of 1968. On July 29, Associated Rediffusion merged with ABC TV (The Associated British Picture Corporation) to form Thames Television, serving the London area on weekdays. Thames TV has produced familiar programs such as *Benny Hill*, *Rumpole of the Bailey*, *Shelley*, and *Executive Stress*. A few days after Thames was established, London Weekend Television was born, taking over broadcasting on the same channel from Friday through Sunday evenings. LWT has created sitcoms such as *Doctor in the House, Bless Me, Father*, and *The Piglet Files*, as well as dramas such as *Upstairs, Downstairs*, and *Agatha Christie's Poirot*. Yorkshire Television also began operations the same week as Thames TV. Some of Yorkshire Television's output seen in America has included the sitcoms *Rising Damp* and *The Bounder*.

By the early 1970s, the British viewing audience's attention was fairly evenly divided between the BBC and ITV. In 1972, Britain's first cable TV station opened in Greenwich, serving 9,000 homes. The introduction of a fourth channel was already being discussed, but it would be another decade before the fourth channel would become a reality. For now, however, let's use this point in the story to celebrate the first Britcom hits of the 1970s.

PART I

"I Didn't Get Where I Am Today..."
Britcoms of the 1970s

DAD'S ARMY

BBC
1968-1977
77 Episodes, 2 Specials

Written by Jimmy Perry and David Croft
Directed by David Croft, Harold Snoad,
  Bob Spiers
Produced by David Croft

Available on home video in the U.S.

Cast:

CAPTAIN MAINWARING .... Arthur Lowe
SERGEANT WILSON .... John Le Mesurier
CORPORAL JONES .... Clive Dunn
PRIVATE GODFREY .... Arnold Ridley
PRIVATE PIKE .... Ian Lavender
PRIVATE WALKER .... James Beck
PRIVATE FRAZER .... John Laurie
ARP WARDEN HODGES .... Bill Pertwee

Dad's Army: Their commitment is unshakable; their competence is questionable. (*Left to right*): Captain Mainwaring (Arthur Lowe), Sergeant Wilson (John Le Mesurier), Corporal Jones (Clive Dunn), Private Frazer (John Laurie), Private Godfrey (Arnold Ridley), Private Pike (Ian Lavender), and Private Walker (James Beck).
BBC Worldwide

Dad's Army was an extremely popular show throughout its long life, and certainly one of the best-loved sitcoms ever created in Britain. It was also the first major hit for writer/producer David Croft. The BBC still reruns the program today (much as *I Love Lucy* is in perpetual reruns on stations across the U.S.).

Set during the Battle of Britain and based on co-creator Jimmy Perry's own experiences with the Local Defense Volunteers, *Dad's Army* takes viewers back to a period of great upheaval when British mettle was put to the test on a daily basis.

The year is 1940. The Germans had begun air raids on England, and the civilians and veteran soldiers of Home Guard are doing their part to defend the Realm. Their job is to scan the skies for incoming planes as well as assist in civil defense emergencies. The heroes of *Dad's Army*, however, are comprised of a motley crew of mostly senior citizens who spend more time getting themselves into awkward predicaments than they do defending their homeland in the war.

The leader of this ragtag bunch is the crabby, pompous Captain Mainwaring, a bank manager by day who has appointed himself head of the Walmington-on-Sea Home Guard platoon. His second-in-command is the laconic Sergeant Wilson, a deputy of unquestioned loyalty yet who also allows Mainwaring to suffer the occasional humiliation to keep his superior officer from feeling *too* superior. The other graying platoon members include the overzealous Corporal Jones (who tends to scurry about shouting, "Don't panic!" at the slightest mishap), the frail Private Godfrey, and the Scottish mortician Private Frazer, purveyor of doom and gloom. The younger men include Mainwaring's nephew Private Pike and black market entrepreneur Private Walker (played by James Beck, who died in 1973 between series 5 and 6). The platoon members meet regularly in a church meeting hall.

In "Don't Forget the Diver," a typical episode filled with clever gags, Mainwaring's men are to compete with the Eastgate platoon in training exercises. Eastgate will guard a windmill while Mainwaring's group will attempt to overtake it. As the plan evolves, it is decided that Corporal Jones will float down the stream by the windmill in a hollowed log, guided underwater by Frazer in a diving suit. As the others work to distract the Eastgate troops, Jones will then make his way across a field and throw a simulated bomb into the windmill to claim victory.

After a run-through in the hall (during which Frazer almost gets the bends in his over-inflated diving suit), the big day arrives. Jones, encased in a large tree trunk borrowed from the local theater, eases downstream with Frazer's help. Meanwhile, Walker has devised a few unlikely but effective diversions, including placing battle helmets on the sheep in the field. The Eastgate lookout men in the windmill are convinced that the sheep are Mainwaring's men in disguise! Jones makes several attempts to hoist himself firmly onto dry land, then encounters a dog that takes an unwelcome liking to the tree trunk. Finally, the determined corporal climbs the windmill ladder, tosses the "bomb" through the window, and declares victory, but the ladder falls, leaving him clinging to the windmill sail until he lets go and lands in the stream from whence he came.

Another episode, "Keeping Young and Beautiful," displays the lengths to which Mainwaring's men will go in the name of loyalty to their leader. The episode opens with a debate in the House of Commons, the issue being the swapping of some older members of the Home Guard with younger men from the Air Raid Patrol. After observing his men go through a disastrous outdoor training session, Captain Mainwaring sees for himself the need to infuse his platoon with some more youthful individuals. However, he doesn't want to discard his older troops and likewise the men don't want to be taken away from their somber but well-meaning leader. The decision is to be made at an upcoming assembly by the area commander.

Upon learning that he himself could be transferred to the ARP, Mainwaring sneaks into his office to try on a less-than-convincing toupee. Wilson suddenly enters and can't suppress his amusement, but then confesses that he's wearing a painfully uncomfortable corset under his uniform. Meanwhile, Jones and Godfrey meet Frazer at his funeral home to ask for a makeup job that might take off a few years. At the assembly, the elder troops stand at attention covered with the mortician's makeup that serves as a poor substitute for the fountain of youth. However, the commander decides not to pick any of them for transfer after all. The platoon's efforts and display of loyalty move Mainwaring, but the poignant moment is interrupted by a cloudburst. The rain wreaks havoc on the men's hair dye and greasy makeup, which runs down their faces as they try to retain their composure.

When Jimmy Perry and David Croft first approached David Mills, then head of comedy at the BBC, with the idea for *Dad's Army*, Mills responded, "This could run forever." And so far, thanks to reruns, it has. *Dad's Army* won the hearts of the viewing public (achieving eighteen million viewers at its peak), as well as winning the BAFTA (British Academy of Film and Television Arts) award for Best Comedy in 1971. A theatrical film version was also released that year. The series reached the end of its run in November of 1977. Columnist Benny Green wrote in *Punch Magazine* at the time, "With *Dad's Army*, [Jimmy Perry] and David Croft managed to pull off a million-to-one trick, the funny show which is also sad . . . that show ran nine years, in the course of which it wriggled into so many hearts. Every character was, of course, clearly and wittily delineated, and nearly every character was well-played."

A Word about David Croft

David Croft could be called the Norman Lear of British television. He has produced and co-written over a half-dozen wildly successful comedy programs in a twenty-year period, beginning with *Dad's Army* and including *Are You Being Served?*, *Hi-De-Hi*, and *'Allo, 'Allo!* He has always preferred writing his sitcoms with a partner; he collaborated with Jimmy Perry on *Dad's Army*, *It Ain't Half Hot, Mum*, *Hi-De-Hi*, and *You Rang, M'Lord?* and worked with Jeremy Lloyd on *Are You Being Served?* and *'Allo, 'Allo!*. "When I started to write *Dad's Army* with Jimmy Perry,"

Croft recalled, "we used to meet for a couple of days, sort out a program each, and go away and write a program each. But after about thirty or forty programs, we started writing face to face." He prefers writing in the same room with someone, provided they get along. "That way we spark the dialogue off between us. Jimmy Perry and Jeremy Lloyd and myself are all actors, and therefore we'd sort of play the parts, and it's worked very well." Croft's comedies are noted for being ensemble shows with large casts playing colorful, eccentric characters, and are usually based on personal experiences or previous means of employment either he or his partners have had in their youth. He has also served as mentor to other directors and producers who have subsequently achieved great success on their own.

A Word about Harold Snoad

Harold Snoad has been one of the most successful comedy producers/directors in the BBC's history. In addition to *Dad's Army*, the most successful programs he has been associated with have been *Are You Being Served?*, *Don't Wait Up*, and *Keeping up Appearances*. He climbed the BBC production ladder in various positions, and became production manager on *Dad's Army*, learning the ropes from David Croft. "David Croft left an awful lot to me, by his own admission," Snoad said, "And he thought I had the skill to do it." Croft then gave Snoad the opportunity to direct a few episodes of the series, which went well. In a practice that is common in Britain but unheard of in America, Snoad later rewrote the TV episodes for a radio version of the series.

The Last of the Summer Wine

BBC
1973–
153 Episodes,
18 Christmas Specials

Produced by Gareth Gwenlan
Written by Roy Clarke

Available on home video in the U.S.

Cast:

COMPO	Bill Owen
CLEGG	Peter Sallis
BLAMIRE	Michael Bates (1973-1976)
FOGGY	Brian Wilde (1976-1986, 1990-)
SEYMOUR	Michael Aldridge (1986-1990)
NORA	Kathy Staff (1973-)

Compo (Bill Owen) continues his relentless pursuit of Nora Batty (Kathy Staff), proving there's no accounting for taste. Looking on are pals Foggy (Brian Wilde) and Clegg (Peter Sallis). *BBC Worldwide*

Among Roy Clarke's many writing accomplishments in television has been his immensely popular series *The Last of the Summer Wine*. Like his *Open All Hours*, it was born as a *Comedy Playhouse* installment in early 1973, and continued as its own series later that year. *Summer Wine* follows the exploits of three old Yorkshire men whiling away their golden years by reminiscing, philosophizing, telling tall tales, and getting into considerable mischief. It has run for over twenty-five years, making it the longest-running sitcom in the world.

Summer Wine spent its first few years playing to a modest audience of about three million. The BBC demonstrated its admirable patience by giving this "slow burner" time to establish an audience. By Christmas of 1981, when it beat *Gone With the Wind* in the ratings, *Summer Wine* was consistently in the top twenty of Britain's favorite programs, with an average audience of about sixteen million.

"[*Summer Wine*] started as a very talky piece," recalled creator/writer Roy Clarke. "It was three characters being somewhat reflective and philosophical and wandering about beautiful scenery. But then, as we went on to the second and third series, I began to pick up where the big laughs were and the feedback I got from the audience, and it almost pushed it into the much broader, fairly heftily slapstick thing that it is now. I find English sitcom audiences, my audiences anyway, certainly seem to like a good deal of visual things."

The most popular and longest-lasting cast lineup consists of Bill Owen, Peter Sallis, and Brian Wilde. Original cast member Michael Bates left the series due to illness, and Wilde left at one point due to personal differences with Owen. When Wilde returned in 1990, viewers rejoiced at having their most beloved triumvirate back intact.

Summer Wine not only has its variety of quietly eccentric characters going for it, but it boasts the beautiful Yorkshire countryside as its backdrop. The majority of each episode was filmed on location in the village of Holmfirth. Roy Clarke said that in the early days of the show, he heard of the village residents watching the broadcasts with the sound off, just to admire the Yorkshire scenery. They later came to appreciate the stories and characters as well.

Clarke used a similar approach in writing *Summer Wine* as he did later for *Open All Hours*. He enjoys allowing each episode's story to unfold at a casual pace. "There's very little plot, certainly

American audiences may not recognize Peter Sallis (Clegg) by sight, but they are more likely to recognize him by sound. He's the voice of Wallace, of the Academy Award-winning *Wallace and Gromit* clay animation comedies.

in the beginning when the series first started. As long as [the audience] was engrossed with the characters it seemed to be okay . . . I realize there's got to be some kind of story, but it's certainly less an emphasis for me than the opportunity of showing the characters at work," he said.

ARE YOU BEING SERVED?

BBC-1
1973-1983
69 Episodes

Written by Jeremy Lloyd and David Croft
Produced by David Croft

Available on home video in the U.S.

Cast:

CAPTAIN PEACOCK	Frank Thornton
MRS. SLOCOMBE	Mollie Sugden
MR. HUMPHRIES	John Inman
MR. GRANGER	Arthur Brough
MR. LUCAS	Trevor Bannister
MISS BRAHMS	Wendy Richard
MR. RUMBOLD	Nicholas Smith
MR. MASH	Larry Martyn
MR. HARMON	Arthur English
YOUNG MR. GRACE	Harold Bennett

Mrs. Slocombe is not amused by the novelty knickers, "and I am unanimous in that." Enjoying a giggle are (*left to right*) Miss Brahms (Wendy Richard), Mr. Lucas (Trevor Bannister), Mr. Rumbold (Nicholas Smith), Mr. Mash (Larry Martyn), Mr. Granger (Arthur Brough), Mr. Humphries (John Inman), and Captain Peacock (Frank Thornton). *BBC Worldwide*

Are You Being Served? is one of the most well-known and popular Britcoms in America, thanks to a great amount of exposure on public television stations throughout the country. As might be expected from the acclaimed writing team of David Croft and Jeremy Lloyd, a typical episode abounds with sight gags and silly situations, and doesn't concern itself too much with a complicated plot. Instead the colorful characters are allowed to amble about and trade wisecracks, wreaking a bit of havoc at Grace Brothers Department Store before confronting the crisis of the day. This gives the series a very casual, airy feel, and before long we come to know the characters as if they are personal friends. Jeremy Lloyd in particular had his earlier experiences as a salesman for a large London department store for a source of material.

Are You Being Served? first aired as a pilot episode in Britain in 1972. It was rushed on the air when the massacre of Israeli athletes at the Munich Olympics temporarily suspended the games, leaving a surplus of television air time. This inauspicious debut for the show received little notice, but the episode was repeated at the beginning of the first regular series in September of 1973 (oddly enough, this episode survives only in black and white). The first series didn't go terribly well according to Harold Snoad. At David Croft's suggestion, Snoad produced and directed the second series. The show became a hit. Snoad said of Croft's reaction, "He said, 'That's absolutely wonderful'— and took it back again! So he continued to do it after that. It didn't worry me because I went on to do other things, but we've had a standing joke about that."

The series opens with the eccentric characters of the Gentlemen's Ready-to-Wear department and Ladies' department quickly establishing their identities. Mr. Granger, a Grace Brothers veteran, has lost a step or two over the years, but still proudly heads the Menswear department. His assistant Mr. Humphries is a cheerful, somewhat flamboyant chap of undetermined age and gender preference. Mr. Lucas is the newest employee, and once he gets his bearings on the job, soon emerges as a fast-talking wiseguy on the make with every attractive female he sees. On the ladies' side, the pompous Mrs. Slocombe, sporting a new hair color (or two) every week, presides over her counter. She's assisted by Miss Brahms, pretty but a tad ditsy, and forever the object of desire for the leering Mr. Lucas. Each department reluctantly shares the floor with the other, and each somehow views the other as a competitor of sorts, despite the fact that they serve different genders. The mediator of their feuds is the stern floorwalker Captain Peacock, who tends to overestimate the importance of his authority, only to have his puffed-up dignity punctured on a regular basis. The floor's supervisor Mr. Rumbold is a dedicated company man, but only a semi-competent one. Then there is the store's founder, Young Mr. Grace, a soft-spoken, frail octogenarian ("Old Mr. Grace doesn't get around much anymore"), who still rules with an iron hand and surrounds himself with young, sexy secretaries and nurses.

It is interesting that the first few episodes of *Are You Being Served?* are seen largely through Mr. Lucas's eyes. He has been on the job only a few weeks, so it makes sense that we learn the workings of Grace Brothers as he does. As Mr. Lucas, Trevor Bannister displays split-second timing and a good deal of comedic spark. And, as the youngest male member of the cast, he is also called upon to perform some of the more challenging slapstick sequences—although the older cast members prove to be in remarkably good shape. Despite the tendency of the earlier episodes to feature Mr. Lucas, it is Mr. Humphries, played with a scene-stealing campiness by John Inman, who becomes a stand-out player in the ensemble and eventually the most popular among viewers. Fortunately, the camaraderie among the cast members never suffers for it.

Aside from the more obvious laughs in *Are You Being Served?*, it is also amusing to note how the third floor of Grace Brothers is chosen as the venue for just about every occasion imaginable, from fire drill practice to play rehearsals to Mrs. Slocombe's ersatz Greek wedding. The staff members are never seen at home, underscoring how the store is the central fixture of their lives.

In the episode "German Week," the store is given an ambiance makeover by way of adding German signs, flags, and music. The staff is expected to enthusiastically push a line of German clothing and products, supposedly to promote goodwill between the two countries. At a staff meeting following a disastrous first day, misgivings about the whole idea bubble to the surface.

Mr. Granger and Mrs. Slocombe in particular recall the days when the British and Germans were deadly enemies. "Some of us have long memories," Mrs. Slocombe angrily points out to Mr. Rumbold. "I'll never forget being flung flat on my back on Clapham Common by a land mine! And the German Air Force was responsible." Mr. Lucas can't resist adding, "All the other times she was flat on her back, the *American* Air Force was responsible!" Despite their protests, the staff dons traditional German costumes and even performs the time-honored knee-slapping dance for Young Mr. Grace. Mrs. Slocombe, inebriated on German wine, gets into a face-slapping exchange with Captain Peacock as the proceeding grinds to a halt.

Early in the episode "Camping In," Mr. Lucas finds himself faced with the task of measuring the inside leg of a kilted Scotsman. Daunted by the idea, he asks Mr. Humphries to do it. "Don't ask me, I've given it up for Lent," Humphries replies. Before long, the staff finds themselves stranded in the store for the night due to a transit strike. With no choice but to get comfortable for the night, Mr. Rumbold suggests they borrow several pup tents from the Outdoors department. The tents are soon erected, but complaints begin to flow in a steady stream. Mrs. Slocombe, despite having the largest tent, voices concern about her privacy against prying eyes. Mr. Mash from Maintenance distributes pajamas borrowed from the Discount department's window mannequins, but Miss Brahms would rather sleep without them. Mrs. Slocombe objects to that idea, noting, "Suppose there was a fire and you had no clothes on?" "Oh, I'd be first to be rescued!" Miss Brahms retorts. Later, in a scene that typifies the unique chemistry among the cast members, we find them all sitting in front of their tents around an electric campfire, singing a wartime song and reminiscing about WWII. Mr. Granger even offers a dubious impersonation of Winston Churchill.

Trevor Bannister, while appearing for an on-air pledge drive for WLIW in New York, made this

On the ladies' side of the floor, Mrs. Slocombe (Mollie Sugden, *right*) gives Miss Brahms (Wendy Richard) the scoop on her latest man-hunt with Mrs. Axelby in the local pub.
BBC Worldwide

interesting observation about the performances in *Are You Being Served?*:

> The sort of show that we were doing, it wasn't what I call pure situation comedy, which involves a much more in-depth writing where people relate one-to-one in the situation. The characters were fairly one-dimensional. . . . There's not an awful lot to hang your hat on, so I think they're very much more personality performances from everybody.

The first of the original cast members to leave the series (besides supporting player Larry Martyn as Mr. Mash) was Arthur Brough, whose wife passed away in the spring of 1978. Brough could not bring himself to continue with his work, and in fact died shortly thereafter. He was replaced by a succession of veteran comedy actors such as James Hayter as Mr. Tebbs, and later Alfie Bass as Mr. Goldberg. In 1979, Trevor Bannister found himself in the position of having to choose between continuing his role as Mr. Lucas or appearing in a touring version of the West End play *Middle-Age Spread*. Feeling that he had done as much as he could with his character, Bannister opted for the play. With yet

another main character to replace on the series, it could be argued that the quality of the show began to falter somewhat from that point on. Mike Berry was brought in to play Mr. Spooner, but his performance lacked Bannister's natural delivery and energy.

John Inman's popularity as Mr. Humphries prompted him to moonlight briefly in 1977 to star in the seven-episode sitcom *Odd Man Out*. In 1981, he starred in the sitcom *Take a Letter, Mr. Jones*. He played Graham Jones, the personal secretary to a female corporate mogul played by Rula Lenska. That series also ran for seven episodes.

Likewise, Mollie Sugden has proven to be a ubiquitous sitcom actress in the years during and following the run of *Are You Being Served?*. She teamed again with David Croft and Jeremy Lloyd in 1978 (in between series of *Served?*) to star in their futuristic farce *Come Back, Mrs. Noah*. Throughout the 1980s, Sugden also starred in more pedestrian domestic sitcoms such as *That's My Boy* and *My Husband and I*, the latter co-starring her real-life husband William Moore.

Perhaps the most surprising role among the former *Are You Being Served?* cast members has been Wendy Richard's portrayal of Pauline Fowler on the top-rated soap opera *EastEnders*. Beginning with the first episode in 1985, Richards has consistently shown herself to be a brilliant dramatic actress, giving her world-weary character great depth and a wide range of emotion. The role is indeed a long way from her earlier days as Miss Brahms, who was never really given much to do on *Served?*.

Most of the *Are You Being Served?* cast reunited with David Croft and Jeremy Lloyd in January of 1992 for the series sequel, *Grace and Favour* (syndicated in America as *Are You Being Served Again?*). In this series, the loyal Grace Brothers staff learns that Young Mr. Grace has left them an old country manor in his will—in lieu of a pension fund. They decide to convert the manor into a hotel. New cast members include the rather coarse groundskeeper Mr. Moultered (Billy Burden) and his beautiful daughter Mavis (Fleur Bennett). Due to limited sleeping accommodations, Mavis has to share a bed with Mr. Humphries! *Grace and Favour* ran for two series of six episodes each.

RISING DAMP

Yorkshire Television
1974-1978
26 Episodes

Written by Eric Chappell
Directed and produced by Ronnie Baxter,
Vernon Lawrence

Available on home video in the U.S.

Cast:

RIGSBY .... Leonard Rossiter
MISS JONES .... Frances de la Tour
ALAN .... Richard Beckinsale
PHILIP .... Don Warrington

Rigsby (Leonard Rossiter),
gives black magic a try,
unaware of his audience, Philip
(Don Warrington) and Alan
(Richard Beckinsale).
Yorkshire Television

Rising Damp was the first of two classic comedy series to showcase the wonderful talents of the late Leonard Rossiter. His performances are still captivating to watch. As Rigsby, the rather crude landlord of a run-down apartment house, Rossiter puts enormous energy into his jittery, hyperactive character. At times, he looks as if he's about to blow some internal gasket, but in fact his mannerisms could run the gamut from the broad to the subtle.

Rising Damp grew from Eric Chappell's 1973 stage play, *The Banana Box*, which starred three of the four TV cast members, except for Richard Beckinsale. The setting and lead character were kept for the TV pilot, but the original name Rooksby was changed to Rigsby when a real-life landlord (and practicing Quaker) named Rooksby complained that he didn't want his reputation to suffer by association!

The idea for the series came from an item Chappell read in the paper about a young African who went to a hotel and impersonated a prince, and was given the royal treatment. For Chappell's creative purposes, the hotel became a seedy boarding house and the story took off from there. As Chappell explained, "I simply wrote the play, and when they said to me, 'Would you like to write it as a television series?' I said, 'Well I don't think I'd have the stamina to write a situation comedy' because I'd only written plays before this. But they persuaded me and I started to write it as a series. Of course it was useful that I had created that situation, but I didn't do it deliberately, no." Chappell had at the same time been developing a sitcom called *The Squirrels*, so he went from never having written a situation comedy to writing two almost simultaneously.

Rising Damp's pilot episode was broadcast in September of 1974 and produced by former *Monty Python* director Ian McNaughton. A full series of *Rising Damp* was ordered shortly thereafter, with Chappell supplying each script for the duration of the show's run.

Rigsby lords over his run-down boarding house with a talent for meddling in the lives of his tenants, and is often the source of their angst. He doesn't hold mankind in especially high esteem, but feels decidedly more charitable towards womankind, especially in the person of his one female tenant, Miss Jones. However, his amorous advances toward her rarely advance very far. His other tenants include Alan, a young medical student, and his roommate Philip, who is in fact a tribal prince in his African homeland. Such a lofty title doesn't impress Rigsby, who doesn't care much for Africans or their descendants anyway, but he is an equal opportunity offender. His insults are usually accompanied by examples of his own puffed-up importance, especially when recounting his experiences in World War II. Whether real or imaginary, his oft-told tales of heroics fuel his sense of superiority over such softies as Alan and Philip.

The boarding house setting for *Rising Damp* allows for additional characters to come and go with varying degrees of frequency. Some tenants appear for a few episodes, and then move on, to be replaced with new arrivals. Like *Fawlty Towers*, this allows for a broader menu of situations for Rigsby and the other permanent characters as they deal with the more transient boarders.

A typical episode has Rigsby confronting one such semi-regular named Spooner, a big, intimidating loudmouth. Spooner is laid up with a broken leg, resulting from having tripped over Rigsby's cat on the stairs. His only entertainment for the time being is his radio, which he plays too loud and late into the night. Miss Jones, Alan, and Philip ask Rigsby to talk with Spooner, since they're too timid to risk irritating him. Rigsby displays his bravado in front of the others, and even drags out his WWII souvenir chest to verify his courage, but he quickly goes soggy when he finds himself alone with Spooner.

In the meantime, Alan has come across a German luger in Rigsby's collection and brings it downstairs to ask him about it. As Rigsby dredges up his war stories about taking the gun from a dead German soldier, he accidentally fires it in the direction of Spooner's door. Fearing the worst, he cautiously opens the door to witness Spooner's motionless body on the couch. Spooner, playing dead, let's everyone but Rigsby in on the joke. He finally puts an end to Rigsby's whimpering, postmortem apologies with a sudden burst of admonishment. The others have a good laugh but the startled Rigsby doesn't find the joke very funny.

Another temporary lodger, Ambrose, features prominently in the episode "Under the Influence." Ambrose is very good at borrowing money but not so good at paying it back. When Rigsby comes calling to collect the rent, Ambrose smoothly changes the subject to elaborate on his claim that he's a mystic gypsy. Soon he's showing off a suitcase full of mysterious devices and exotic potions to the mocking Rigsby, who takes an interest in the "sexometer" used to measure the user's romantic prowess. Ambrose later attempts to demonstrate his hypnotic skills to a skeptical Philip, but succeeds only in sending an unsuspecting Rigsby into a trance. Miss Jones enters to find her landlord sitting in his underwear (thanks to Ambrose and his powers of persuasion), and hurries out, leaving Rigsby to tend to some damage control.

Rigsby holds Ambrose responsible for the misunderstanding. In an attempt to make amends, Ambrose hypnotizes Rigsby again, giving him the persona of a great lover irresistible to women. Rigsby's newfound aggressiveness toward Miss Jones is met with a pie in his face (her only handy defense). He later decides that it's *Miss Jones* who should be hypnotized. Ambrose reluctantly puts her under (or so he thinks) and soon she is attacking the surprised Rigsby with a passion that even he can't handle. The romantically confused Rigsby rejects hypnotism in favor of a Humphrey Bogart-style approach. Assuming he's been hypnotized yet again, Miss Jones responds with a squirt of seltzer in his face. Ambrose arrives, and agrees to save the humiliated Rigsby—for the modest fee of ten pounds. To demonstrate that Rigsby is actually under a spell, Ambrose stomps on Rigsby's foot and encourages Miss Jones to stick him with a hatpin, which she does. The unflinching Rigsby waits until he's safely out on the stairwell before letting out his scream.

Leonard Rossiter has been acknowledged by those who worked on *Rising Damp*, as having been the driving force behind the series. He even instilled a bit of fear with his no-nonsense approach to rehearsing and impatience with frivolous suggestions. Veteran television and stage actor Peter Bowles appeared in several episodes of *Rising Damp* as Hilary, an unemployed actor. He has clear memories of having worked with his old friend Rossiter:

> You know you have very little time on these sitcoms, so people mainly want you to get on with the lines and not come up with too many ideas of your own. Anyway, I came up with an idea, and everybody ducked for cover and sort of hid behind chairs, but Leonard said 'That's a terrific idea, come on let's do it.' And that's really what I remember working with Leonard, and also how extraordinarily professional he was in that when he came into rehearsals. He wouldn't stand around having a cup of coffee and chatting. He would walk straight into the middle of the rehearsal room and start speaking.

Rising Damp won the BAFTA for Best Comedy in 1976, one of the first ITV shows to do so. A feature film version written by Eric Chappell was produced in 1980, and won Frances de la Tour the *Evening Standard*'s Best Actress Award.

After *Rising Damp*, Frances de la Tour starred in a short-lived series called *Flickers*, set in the early days of motion pictures. The show was written by Roy Clarke (*Open All Hours, Keeping up*

Remembered for his serious approach to comic acting, Leonard Rossiter allows himself a laugh on the set. *Yorkshire Television*

Appearances) and co-starred Bob Hoskins (*Who Framed Roger Rabbit?*) who was yet to achieve renown as a versatile dramatic and comic actor.

Richard Beckinsale, like Leonard Rossiter, performed double-duty throughout most of *Rising Damp*'s run. Beginning in 1976, Rossiter appeared simultaneously in *Rising Damp* and *The Fall and Rise of Reginald Perrin*. Beckinsale co-starred with Ronnie Barker in the BBC hit *Porridge*, which ran concurrently with *Rising Damp* for three years. Sadly, Beckinsale died of a heart attack in March of 1979 while starring in a new sitcom, *Bloomers*. Production ceased altogether upon his untimely death.

A WORD ABOUT ERIC CHAPPELL

Series creator and writer Eric Chappell has written no fewer than ten sitcoms, mostly for Yorkshire Television, since the early 1970s. His hits, in addition to *Rising Damp* have included *Only When I Laugh* and *The Bounder*. He still writes sitcom pilots but confesses his true love is writing theatrical plays.

Gorden Kaye (star of *'Allo,'Allo!*) said, "I was very fond of *Rising Damp*. That fine performer Leonard Rossiter was one of the best."

FAWLTY TOWERS

BBC-2
12 Episodes
1975, 1979

The courteous and helpful staff of Fawlty Towers: *(clockwise from top)* Basil (John Cleese), Polly (Connie Booth), Manuel (Andrew Sachs), and Sybil (Prunella Scales). *BBC Worldwide*

Written by John Cleese and Connie Booth
Directed by John Howard Davies (series 1)
*   Bob Spiers (series 2)*
Produced by John Howard Davies (series 1)
*   Douglas Argent (series 2)*

Available on home video in the U.S.

Cast:

BASIL FAWLTY	John Cleese
SYBIL FAWLTY	Prunella Scales
MANUEL	Andrew Sachs
POLLY	Connie Booth

Once in a great while, the entertainment world bestows upon a new film or television show the lofty status of "instant classic" upon its premiere, and universal acclaim over time ensures the work's place in entertainment history. In television, few situation comedies have deserved the "instant classic" label as much as *Fawlty Towers*, created by ex-Python John Cleese and his wife at the time, Connie Booth. There isn't much that can be said about this show that hasn't already been said in the past twenty years. The series has been praised as a comedy milestone by fans and television professionals alike. And the *Fawlty Towers* comedy legacy is all the more remarkable when considering that the entire output of the program consisted of a mere 12 episodes.

According to legend, the idea for *Fawlty Towers* grew from an actual experience by Cleese and his fellow Pythons at a hotel while filming on location near Torquay. The hotel manager apparently made no effort to mask his disdain for his guests. A few years later, Cleese left Python and planned to collaborate more with Connie Booth. When the BBC approached him to do a new series, it didn't take long to hit upon the premise of a hotel setting featuring a relentlessly rude manager. "It was the second or third idea that came into our minds."

The first series of six episodes began in September of 1975, when viewers were first introduced to the manic Basil Fawlty, his shrewish wife Sybil, their hopelessly incompetent Spanish waiter Manuel, and their level-headed, sarcastic housekeeper Polly. Prunella Scales as Sybil and Andrew Sachs as Manuel are standouts in their roles.

John Cleese offers his explanation (to Melvyn Bragg, host of *The South Bank Show*) on how an incorrigible character like Fawlty could prove so popular:

> I think one of the reasons why Basil
> Fawlty was a very successful creation

was that he embodied a kind of thing that the English feel sometimes, which is that they can't say, 'I'm sorry, this food is not good enough' or 'I bought this pair of shoes and I want you to replace it' because they can't do these simple acts of self-assertion. They tend to become on the surface a kind of brittle politeness and underneath a lot of seething rage. And I think that so many people in England feel this that that was one of the reasons they could identify with Basil, also find him funny and at the same time quite like him . . . he's a monster! And yet people feel quite affectionately about him, which is a very strange paradox.

Of course, before a program can be taped, aired, and in this case praised, it must be written. And therein lies the key to *Fawlty Towers*'s extraordinary creative success and mass popularity. Cleese has always been especially proud of the scripts and the scriptwriting process he and Booth went through for each episode. While most sitcom episodes are written in a week to ten days, Cleese and Booth took an average of six weeks to construct each episode. They would sit with a large sheet of drawing paper and jot down ideas for a beginning or middle of a story, making short notes off to the side, and ever-so-slowly construct the plot over a two-week period. He explains their technique:

On *Fawlty Towers* Connie and I used to spend enormous quantities of time on the plot . . . there were certain things we took pride in, trying not to let the audience guess what was going to happen. So whenever we were getting plot points across or establishing something that was absolutely necessary to lead on to the final direction of the story, we would always try to make it as funny as possible so that people thought it had been put in because it was funny, but at the same time they would absorb the point, the plot point. . . . We would try to get two or three threads and at a particular point . . . basically they start on

separate tracts and then start weaving. And of course the best ones are where they all come together right at the end. . . . Connie and I would laugh till the tears rolled down our faces, but we would always ache for Basil. We were really like two gods—we were writing this man's life and making it absolutely awful—he never had a chance!

Cleese has described his Monty Python sketches, mostly written with the late Graham Chapman, as having relied a bit more on verbal comedy (and *Roget's Thesaurus*), while Michael Palin and Terry Jones preferred a visual, almost cinematic quality to many of their contributions. However, he was no doubt speaking in the most general of terms, because the breathless, high energy slapstick of *Fawlty Towers* underlines his true versatility as a comic writer and visual performer. While the dialogue is no less capable of providing big laughs, it is probably the visual quality of the comedy that makes the biggest impression. Cleese himself maintains that a great visual gag stays with the viewer much longer than the dialogue.

While fans may be quick to claim that each and every *Fawlty Towers* episode is a classic, some are obviously better than others. Highlight episodes include, from the first series, "Gourmet Night" and "The Germans."

In "Gourmet Night" we find Basil pursuing his relentless quest to attract a higher class of clientele. He arranges a formal dinner to feature his new chef, Kurt. The first setback occurs when most of the guests must cancel at the last moment, leaving just two couples in attendance. Basil decides to make do, until Polly informs him that Kurt has drunk himself into a stupor (apparently Manuel has rejected his affectionate advances). With no dinner to serve, the panic-stricken Basil hurries into town to pick up a prefab duck dinner at his friend Andre's restaurant. Back in the hotel kitchen, he and Manuel collide as Manuel's foot wedges its way into the duck. A second mad dash back to Andre's follows, where Basil thinks he's picking up a new duck dinner (it is obscured by a silver tray cover). His car stalls on the way back, bringing on an apoplectic fit as he screams at the car and even beats it with a tree branch. Finally, he wheels the dinner into the dining room and lifts the silver lid

"Duck's off, sorry." Basil (John Cleese) presents an unexpected main course to his honored guests in "Gourmet Night." *BBC Worldwide*

from the tray to reveal a large trifle dessert. The impatient guests are not amused. "Duck's off, sorry," he says meekly.

"The Germans" opens with Sybil in the hospital to have an ingrown toenail removed. Basil is left to manage on his own. He announces to the guests that he will soon be conducting a fire drill, but it proves to be beyond his abilities. The confused guests bombard him with increasingly infuriating questions as he attempts to demonstrate the proper procedure. At the height of the confrontation, Manuel bursts into the lobby from the kitchen to announce a real fire, only to be dismissed by Basil and sent back into the smoke-filled room. Andrew Sachs suffered real burns while taping the scene, and was compensated for his injuries.

Later, after receiving a nasty bump on the head, Basil finds himself sharing Sybil's hospital room. Woozy from a concussion but concerned about the hotel, he "escapes" in time to welcome the long-awaited German guests. Despite his admonishments to Polly "not to mention the war," the light-headed Basil promptly upsets his guests with several ugly references to Nazi Germany. As memorable as this episode is (in 1997 it was ranked number twelve in *TV Guide*'s list of the 100 greatest episodes of all time), Cleese himself was less than totally satisfied with it, conceding that the two halves don't fit together very well.

There is a noticeable gap of time between production of the first and second series. One reason is that Cleese and the other members of Monty

Python began writing the script for their feature film, *The Life of Brian*. More significantly, Cleese and Connie Booth divorced. Despite the obvious emotional strain, they shared the desire to continue working together as writing partners. In February of 1979 a new series of six *Fawlty Towers* episodes began its run. Cleese feels the second series is stronger than the first. Certainly, two episodes in particular rank as classics.

"The Kipper and the Corpse" provides Basil with a hotelier's nightmare—a dead guest. In this case, an ill guest retires for the evening and asks to have his breakfast sent up the following morning. Basil resents the inconvenience but delivers the breakfast and chats away, oblivious to the fact that the guest is as dead as a door nail. Polly discovers the body, and Basil embarks on a mission to get the body out of the room and out of sight of the guests until the undertaker arrives. He and a reluctant Manuel drag the body through hallways and into closets and laundry baskets. At one point, the elderly Mrs. Tibbs catches sight of the corpse and faints dead away, leaving Basil with two bodies to shuffle about the hotel.

The absurd slapstick ballet of "The Kipper and the Corpse" is perhaps surpassed by the final episode of the series, "Basil the Rat." A surprise visit by the health inspector puts the staff on notice. Everything in the hotel must be spotless in time for his follow-up visit. Later, Basil discovers Manuel has been keeping a pet rat, which has to go. During the inspector's next visit, the rat returns (Manuel has been secretly keeping it in a storage barn). Rat poison ends up on a piece of veal, possibly on the dish served to the inspector. A tangle of complications ensues, topped off with a frantic chase after the rat through several rooms of the hotel. It disappears momentarily, only to reappear sitting in a tin of biscuits offered to the inspector. His face-to-face meeting with the rat leaves him in a daze, as Manuel drags the unconscious Basil out of the dining room.

This episode aired nearly seven months after the rest of the series, due to a union strike at the BBC. (John Cleese had wanted Basil's final appearance to be in a sketch for the premiere episode of *Not The Nine O'Clock News*. Instead, this final episode aired on its own shortly thereafter.)

It is on the strength of such perfectly crafted episodes like these that *Fawlty Towers* has risen so far above the usual standard for situation comedies. It does not stand alone, but it has become the unofficial measuring stick against which later farcical sitcoms have been judged.

The end of *Fawlty Towers* only brought more work for the cast members in various roles on television and in films. American viewers have seen Prunella Scales in the popular ten-part series *Mapp and Lucia*, a comedy of manners co-starring Geraldine McEwan and Nigel Hawthorne (*Yes, Minister*). Andrew Sachs has a lengthy list of TV and film roles to his credit, including the *Are You Being Served?* feature film (in which he plays a Spanish hotel manager). American viewers have also seen Sachs in the title role in the 1996 docudrama *Einstein*. John Cleese in particular has kept a high profile since his days as Basil Fawlty. He continued directing and co-starring in the *Secret Policeman's Ball* series of sketch comedy shows for charity. The shows have featured the top music and comedy performers in Britain, and have been seen in the United States on film and on cable television. In 1983 he again teamed with his fellow Pythons for their last feature film, *The Meaning of Life*, which, due to several scenes of dubious taste, managed to offend almost as many people as *The Life of Brian* had.

Cleese delved further into films with a role in the American western *Silverado*, but found a role perfectly suited for him in the 1986 British feature *Clockwise*. Written by Michael Frayn (author of the highly-praised stage comedy *Noises Off*), the film stars Cleese as an uptight schoolmaster who rules his life with obsessive punctuality. His rigid lifestyle falls apart the day he misses his train to an important national conference, forcing him to go to any lengths to arrive on time.

Cleese's most popular screen project so far has been *A Fish Called Wanda*, a farce he wrote and co-directed in 1988 with veteran Charles Chricton and co-starring Jamie Lee Curtis, Kevin Kline, and Michael Palin. The cast reunited for the film *Fierce Creatures*, released in January of 1997.

For all of his post-*Fawlty Towers* successes, however, John Cleese will most likely always be associated with that rude, hyperkinetic hotel owner who routinely manages to create disaster for himself within the confines of his otherwise quiet little inn. It's not a bad legacy for a comedy writer/performer who puts such care into his art.

David Renwick (creator/writer of *One Foot in the Grave*): "To me the really innovative comedy show was *Fawlty Towers*. It just stands there as a great beacon to me . . . I don't think there have been many other shows that have taken up where that left off. And that was twenty years ago."

Andrew Norriss (creator/writer of *The Brittas Empire*): "The thing I liked most about *Fawlty Towers* was that complication of the plotting, the way facts are fed in very early on and then reappear later on and they all come together . . . it's genius what they did, John Cleese and Connie."

Good Neighbors (The Good Life)

BBC
1975-1978
30 Episodes

Written by John Esmonde and Bob Larbey
Produced by John Howard Davies

Available on home video in the U.S.

Cast:

Tom Good	Richard Briers
Barbara Good	Felicity Kendal
Margo Leadbetter	Penelope Keith
Jerry Leadbetter	Paul Eddington

Good neighbors and the best of friends. (*Left to right*) Barbara Good (Felicity Kendal), Tom Good (Richard Briers), Margo Leadbetter (Penelope Keith), and Jerry Leadbetter (Paul Eddington).
BBC Worldwide

Good Neighbors best represents the quintessential domestic Britcom of the 1970s. It also boasts a special charm of its own due in great part to its legendary cast. All four of the stars went on to great success in their respective careers, especially on television, and remain extremely popular in their own right with the British public.

Good Neighbors, known in the United Kingdom as *The Good Life*, places two households side by side with a world of difference between the home owners. Tom Good, once a draftsman for a company that manufactures toys for cereal boxes, has quit his job and rejected capitalism and all that it stands for. With the support of his devoted wife Barbara, he has taken the big and daunting step of beginning a new life by living via self-sufficiency. They are to grow all of their own food, replace money with the barter system, and sacrifice most of life's luxuries. Tom wouldn't have blamed his wife if she left him outright, but she has instead rolled up

her sleeves to work alongside her husband in their miniature backyard farm. Together, they face problems that the average suburban homeowner couldn't imagine, but they never allow themselves to take life too seriously. In fact, they rarely take anything seriously for very long.

The Goods' well-to-do next-door neighbors and best friends, Jerry and Margo Leadbetter, are by contrast perfectly content with life's luxuries. Margo is a status-conscious snob who has little patience for fools. She is also uptight and easily embarrassed, making her a perfect foil for Tom and Barbara's giddy, prankish behavior. She cannot comprehend their lifestyle, especially how Barbara can actually get her hands dirty each day and live without updating her wardrobe regularly. Jerry Leadbetter, once a work colleague of Tom's, doesn't enjoy the rat race any more than Tom did but knows his wife well enough to keep his job secure and checkbook healthy or face dire consequences. He too thinks the

Goods are a bit daft for choosing the life they have, but he respects their earnestness and their tireless efforts to make it work. The differing lifestyles between the two couples provide splendid fun throughout the series, and Penelope Keith's portrayal of the stuffy Margo often steals the show with her disapproving attitude.

Richard Briers gives writers John Esmonde and Bob Larbey the credit they deserve. He said, "I hate the vacuous and the cheap. And they're not like that. They don't go after cheap laughs. They're dedicated to the truth of human behavior. It's like holding up a mirror, and if what we see is rather funny and rather pathetic then I think perhaps the answer is that we are all rather funny and rather pathetic."

In "The Happy Event," Tom and Barbara prepare for their pig to give birth. The big moment unfortunately occurs in the middle of the night, and the Leadbetters soon find themselves assisting midwife Tom in the pigpen. Margo is both annoyed at the inconvenience and repulsed by the multiple piglet births. After piglet number seven arrives she whines, "Oh, surely seven is enough!" The excitement of the event is marred by the last arrival, a runt that appears to be too small and weak to survive. Tom's practical attitude to just let it die infuriates Barbara, who bullies him into a change of heart. All four promptly begin an emergency procedure to save the runt. Jerry and Barbara, still in their bathrobes, head to the nearest hospital to borrow an oxygen tank, only to be stopped by a motorcycle cop for speeding. The cop, seeing the middle-aged man and his young, pretty companion in their bathrobes, is understandably suspicious of the situation, but when they explain their mission of mercy, he quickly offers his help. Back at home, Tom and Margo spoon-feed the piglet and assemble a makeshift oxygen tent. Their efforts pay off, and the piglet pulls through.

"The Windbreak War" brings the Goods and Leadbetters to near-fighting words. Just as Tom and Barbara plant several rows of fruit plants in their yard, Margo erects a windbreak which casts a life-threatening shadow over the plants. She agrees to have it moved, but the builders fail to see the note instructing them to do so. Furious over Margo's apparently spiteful ways, the Goods decide to have the last laugh by replanting everything away from the windbreak. The only trouble is that Margo has ordered her workmen to move the windbreak as they had failed to do so before. Now

that both neighbors' "corrections" have left them where they started, a confrontation follows, during which they all realize how communications broke down. Once reconciled, Tom invites himself and Barbara to dinner at the Leadbetters, and even offers to bring a bottle of his homemade wine.

The following scenes are a treat, and are only possible with such clearly defined characters. Jerry and Barbara, both quite a bit tipsy from the wine, begin to clean up in the kitchen, where Jerry reveals his secret crush on her. "Jerry, I'm a married woman," Barbara warns. "Well, so am I," he answers. But they both agree that wife-swapping just wouldn't be proper. In the living room, an equally tipsy Margo confesses to Tom that she wishes she had a sense of humor, so she wouldn't have to be the constant butt of jokes. Tom consoles her that not only is she fun to be around, but throws in the observation, "You have a very sexy neck." His babbling sweet talk is interrupted by Jerry and Barbara's reappearance. They all end the evening by moving the windbreak in the yard yet again, falling about laughing and quite drunk—including Margo, who finally gets to share in the laughter.

Perhaps the series' funniest episode is "I Talk to the Trees." Tom and Barbara chat with a kindly old man who talks to his greenhouse plants and plays music for them to keep them happy and healthy. Although skeptical at first, the Goods decide to duplicate the experiment at home. Using newly planted beans as the subjects, with each one under its own plastic cover, Tom instructs Barbara to speak sweetly to one bean, after which he'll spew verbal venom onto the other. He'll compare their growth in the following days. Barbara can barely keep a straight face throughout her sweet-talking performance. "Well, I mean," she giggles, "it's a bean, isn't it?" But she finds her groove, and romances the bean as Tom looks on with considerable bemusement. "Who were you thinking of?" he demands to know. The experiment continues as he dusts off an old record player to fill the air with a truly hokey song called 'The Bandolero' sung by crooner Peter Dawson. After a few days, the experiment appears to show positive results, and Barbara has even named her bean Douglas.

In the meantime, Margo hosts a meeting of the music society in her home. As part of her candidacy for president, she offers to make her home the permanent meeting place for the group. She

Tom and Barbara have a talent for whisking their predicaments into the Leadbetters' living room. *BBC Worldwide*

even offers a contribution from Jerry's checkbook to sweeten the pot, and emphasizes the spacious, quiet surroundings her home affords, making it perfectly suitable for rehearsals. Just then, the strains of 'The Bandolero' waft through the French doors, so unnerving Margo that she stomps furiously into the Goods' living room/laboratory. Her tirade exposes Barbara's beloved Douglas Bean to verbal abuse, thus ruining the experiment. Tom and Barbara berate her for her tirade, just as Jerry arrives with the news that Margo has won the music society election. She offers to make amends with the Goods by having Jerry write a check for any damages. "My function, you know," he sighs.

In this standout episode, Felicity Kendal's mild case of laryngitis during that week of taping adds an unexpectedly endearing touch. She can barely force some of her lines out!

Interestingly enough, the part of Jerry Leadbetter was originally to be played by Peter Bowles (who would eventually get to play opposite Penelope Keith in *To the Manor Born* and *Executive Stress*). Although Bowles was keen to be part of the show, he explains how and why that didn't happen:

> At the same time I was offered a play called *Absent Friends* by Alan Ayckbourn. And I hadn't done a stage play for eleven years, and I decided that I wanted to do a stage play and I wanted to do a comedy. So I decided I would do the stage play. When I arrived at rehearsal, there was Richard Briers. He said to me, 'Why did you turn down *The*

Good Life? The scripts are wonderful.' And I said, 'I know they're wonderful, but I couldn't do it because I'm doing this play.' And he said, 'Didn't anybody tell you that they record the show on Sundays?' And they hadn't [told me]. And so the play ran a year, during which time they did two recordings of *The Good Life* and repeats. And Richard was always banging on my dressing room door showing me his pay slips.

Briers doesn't recall teasing Bowles to quite that degree, however he did impress upon his friend that regular television work, such as a sitcom, offers considerable financial rewards.

In 1977, during a break from taping the series, Briers and Penelope Keith co-starred in a Thames TV production of Alan Ayckbourn's comedy trilogy, *The Norman Conquests* (which also starred Tom Conti).

As noted earlier, all of the cast members of *Good Neighbors* went on to further television success after the show completed production in 1978. Keith reappeared the following year to star in the tremendously popular *To The Manor Born*, for which she won several awards (to add to those she had won for *Good Neighbors*). This in turn was followed by her starring roles in *Executive Stress, No Job for a Lady*, and *Next of Kin*. Briers returned to TV in the sitcoms *All in Good Faith, Ever Decreasing Circles* (written by *Good Neighbors* writers John Esmonde and Bob Larbey), and the short-lived *Down to Earth* (with 'Allo, 'Allo! alumnus Kirsten Cooke). He even wrote a book in 1981 called *Natter, Natter*, in which he offers advice on the art of conversation. In 1989, he received the OBE (Order of the British Empire) from Queen Elizabeth. Felicity Kendal starred in two further series, *Solo* and *The Mistress*, both written by quasi-feminist comedy writer Carla Lane. And, of course, Paul Eddington hit paydirt as Jim Hacker in *Yes, Minister* and *Yes, Prime Minister*. All of these excellent comic actors well deserved their subsequent Britcom triumphs in the decade following their collaboration on *Good Neighbors*.

Queen Elizabeth herself once attended a taping of *Good Neighbors*.

OPEN ALL HOURS

BBC-2, BBC-1
1976, 1979-1982
25 Episodes

Written by Roy Clarke
Produced and directed by Sydney Lotterby

Available on home video in the U.S.

Cast:

ARKWRIGHT . . . . Ronnie Barker
GRANVILLE . . . . David Jason
NURSE GLADYS EMMANUEL . . . . . Lynda Baron

The Arkwright Empire, such as it is. (*Left to right*): Nurse Gladys Emanuel (Lynda Baron), Arkwright (Ronnie Barker), and Granville (David Jason). *BBC Worldwide*

Open All Hours owes most of its appeal to the talents of two veteran comedy performers, Ronnie Barker and David Jason. Both were already household names when they joined forces for this series written by Roy Clarke. Barker was a regular on David Frost's *The Frost Report* in the mid-1960s, and later teamed with fellow Frost performer Ronnie Corbett for the long-running *Two Ronnies* comedy/variety series. He also starred in the popular sitcom *Porridge*, which overlapped somewhat with the first series of *Open All Hours*.

David Jason, a contemporary of the Monty Python troupe, starred with Michael Palin, Terry Jones, and Eric Idle in the comedy sketch program *Do Not Adjust Your Set* in 1968. He also had his own series, *The Top Secret Life of Edgar Briggs*, in which he played an inept Secret Service agent. He had already been good friends with Barker at this point, since they worked together on another show, *Hark At Barker*.

Open All Hours was written for Barker and began as an installment of *Comedy Playhouse*, the BBC's popular showcase for comedy writers. As creator/writer Roy Clarke recalled, "It was tailor-made for Ronnie Barker. It arose from an idea the BBC had some years ago. They did six half-hour sitcom pilots all for Ronnie Barker, from which they hoped some would at least spin off into a series, one of which was *Porridge*, and the other one was *Open All Hours*." From there, the first series of six episodes were produced and ran on BBC-2 in 1976. They were rerun on BBC-1 in 1979, where the show caught on with audiences in a big way.

Barker plays Arkwright, a cynical, penny-pinching shopkeeper with a pronounced stammer whose corner general store is his kingdom and his life. He lives with and rules over his nephew Granville who is of undetermined age but is still waiting for his first meaningful encounter with a mature woman. Arkwright has somehow decided that such life experiences would do Granville more harm than good, so he does his best to keep a tight reign on his ambitious nephew. At the same time, Arkwright easily distracts himself with impure thoughts of his fiancée, the ample nurse Gladys Emmanuel, who lives across the street with her mother. Although they are engaged in some vague way, nurse Gladys puts up fair resistance to the shopkeeper's lustful advances.

The plot of each episode takes its time to develop, and even when it does, it tends to take a back seat to the characters themselves and how they relate to each other. "I'm afraid I am very character-oriented at the expense of plot, probably often," confessed Roy Clarke, who has always preferred character comedy over the strictly situational type of comedy. "I find they last longer, and I find what people ultimately, it seems to me, latch onto is characters that they like, and if they take a character in, they're happy to follow them," he said. This gives viewers time to learn about the characters and what thoughts occupy them on any given day. Granville in particular is wont to philosophize about life in general, and what it might be like to live the more glamorous life of a famous singer or movie star. "Do you believe that there is a destiny that shapes our ends?" he wonders aloud to his uncle. Arkwright, not one to take such matters seriously, replies, "If the average man had been responsible for shaping his own end, then things would have turned out a lot better looking." Granville also asks persistent questions about the parents he never knew. His late mother (Arkwright's sister) apparently gave new meaning to the word promiscuous. The unknown father was possibly of royal Hungarian lineage, a notion that on occasion fills Granville with a heightened if fleeting sense of self-importance.

Each episode features the snappy interplay between the two characters, as well as between them and their customers. Arkwright tries everything in the book to persuade his clientele to make that one extra purchase. When sweet talk fails, he'll enlist Granville to perform not-so-subtle psychological maneuvers, such as standing by a new crateload of apples, avidly munching one under the nose of a targeted customer. A few of the many brainstorms designed to improve business have included a self-service section in the store (which fails when Arkwright realizes he doesn't trust customers to serve themselves), and a delivery truck/mobile store, converted from a rickety ice cream truck (which incinerates itself on its maiden voyage). One day, he surprises one of his regular customers with the sign "Free Gift With Every Purchase." The "gift," he explains, is in fact the brown paper bag into which he's just placed the grocery order.

David Jason's gift for visual comedy highlights many episodes. One memorable moment comes during a rainstorm, which inspires him to mimic Gene Kelly's splash-filled sequence in *Singing in the Rain*. Jason gives it the full treatment, with a few additional comic touches. In other episodes, he makes the most of the sequences in which he delivers his goods by bicycle throughout the town. He once finds a pair of legs belonging to a discarded mannequin and takes them along, finding uses for them that cause a number of double takes from those passing by.

Another memorable but virtually plotless episode concludes with a location sequence loaded with sight gags. It all begins innocently enough in the predawn hours, just as Granville and Arkwright open for the day. Arkwright and nurse Gladys will be attending her niece's wedding later that day, but he decides to pay his fiancée an early morning visit anyway. With the help of the reluctant Granville, he climbs a ladder to Gladys's bedroom window to admire her in her nightgown. As usual, she considers his innuendoes ill-timed, and slams the window on his hand (he is actually lucky this time; he's been known to come crashing down on the ladder in other visits to his fiancée's window). The episode continues at a leisurely pace but includes several fun scenes, including one in which Arkwright and Granville have trouble communicating with a motorcyclist who can't seem to lift up the tinted visor of his helmet.

Later, Granville irons Arkwright's trousers and laments about his trouble meeting women, but doesn't get any sympathy from his uncle. Arkwright and Gladys set off for the wedding in the country, but his old suit carries such a heavy stench of mothballs that Gladys insists he hold it out the car window on the way. Later, they stop at the side of the road so he can put it back on but his pants still reek, and he's soon clumsily removing them in the car. On the road once again, the billowing pants fly off the roof rack and into the face of a motorcyclist behind them. Arkwright, seeing the motorcyclist discard the pants, has to pull over and retrieve them. But just then a farm tractor lumbers by, its muddy wheels running over the pants and leaving Arkwright trouserless for the wedding. A shot of him and Gladys in the chapel reveals that Gladys, still wearing her overcoat, has loaned him her polyester slacks for the remainder of the day.

Each episode ends late at night with a high-angle shot of Arkwright outside the shop, as he moves the sidewalk displays back inside. In a wistful voice-over we hear him reflecting on the events of the day, ending with a pithy remark to sum it all up.

The series' exterior scenes were shot in Thorne, Doncaster, which coincidentally is the hometown of Roy Clarke's wife. "My wife at one time ran a small shop in a small Yorkshire town," he added, "and so I had a certain feeling of confidence in the background of the [series] because of that." The first series' episodes were adapted into short story form by Christine Sparks in 1976.

Ronnie Barker thoroughly enjoyed his role as Arkwright. As he told talk show host Terry Wogan, "I adored playing [*Porridge*], of course I did. But actually playing *Open All Hours* was somehow a bit more fun. He's a bit more zany, a bit more daft."

Barker's former partner Ronnie Corbett has also offered high praise for *Open All Hours*, calling it "a rich creation . . . the [speech] impediment, and the brown coat, and David Jason—very, very richly

comic and complete people. They both are. And it was just a wonderful series."

Upon the completion of *Open All Hours*, Ronnie Barker began to curtail much of his television work and eventually eased into retirement, partly due to his doctor's advice (Barker had high blood pressure). He also felt that there just wasn't enough quality material to work with. In 1988, at the ripe old age of fifty-eight, he made his official retirement announcement on Terry Wogan's talk show. "I've been very lucky," he told Wogan, "I've done everything I've wanted to do . . . and so, why not? Enjoy yourself." As Gorden Kaye (star of *'Allo, 'Allo!*) recalled, "Ronnie retired a few years ago, and everybody thought it would last six months and he'd come back, but he didn't. Surprised us all."

Barker had another surprise in store. After spending the next decade quietly running an antique shop with his wife Joy in Chipping Norton, Oxfordshire, Barker's name resurfaced. It was announced in August of 1997 that he had been coerced by the BBC to return in a series of specials, to coincide with the BBC's 75th anniversary.

While Barker was content to relax with his OBE medal (awarded by Queen Elizabeth in 1978) and his three BAFTA awards, David Jason found continued success with several series. In *The Darling Buds of May*, he played the patriarch of a Yorkshire family in the 1950s. There was initially some controversy surrounding the series because his character and the "wife" weren't technically married. But the series achieved great popularity regardless. Jason followed this success with an even greater one, starring in the highly praised and enormously popular comedy *Only Fools and Horses*. The versatile Jason, who won his own BAFTA in 1988, has more recently starred in the drama series, *A Touch of Frost*.

The Fall and Rise of Reginald Perrin

BBC
1976-1979
21 Episodes

Reggie (Leonard Rossiter), moments before another train commute to Sunshine Desserts.
BBC Worldwide

Written by David Nobbs
Directed by and produced by John Howard Davies (pilot), Gareth Gwenlan (series)

Cast:

Reginald Perrin	Leonard Rossiter
Elizabeth Perrin	Pauline Yates
C. J.	John Barron
Joan	Sue Nicholls
Tony Webster	Trevor Adams
David Harris-Jones	Bruce Bould

As a companion piece to his successful role as Rigsby in *Rising Damp*, Leonard Rossiter's portrayal of Reginald Perrin became his best-known role and crowning achievement, further demonstrating his brilliance. It is unfortunate that he is no longer around to delight us with his breathtaking comic acting. He died in November of 1984 while starring in yet another sitcom, *Tripper's Day*.

David Nobbs originally created Reginald Perrin for his book *The Death of Reginald Perrin*, which he then adapted for the series at the request of the BBC. Reggie is a forty-six-year-old executive for Sunshine Desserts, a company that has seen better days. And so, apparently, has Reggie. The first few episodes in particular offer an unforgettable mixture of hilarious comedy and the study of a man sinking unmistakably into the depths of depression and nervous exhaustion. Rarely has the portrayal of such a breakdown been as funny as it

is poignant. As Reggie, Leonard Rossiter's jittery manner and quick delivery perfectly capture a man coming apart at the seams. But he also slows down and stops, with increasing frequency, to daydream about such fantasies as seducing his secretary Joan on his desktop in the middle of an open field. These bizarre blackouts usually occur right in the middle of the dialogue, with a quick cut to Reggie's faraway grin, and are delightful in their unexpected appearances. He clearly would rather be anywhere else in the world other than in his office, marketing new desserts. His overbearing, half-crazed boss C. J. is given to making pronouncements beginning with, "I didn't get where I am today by . . ." C. J.'s variations of the line tend to become increasingly long-winded, depending on the subject at hand.

Reggie's home life is tedious to him as well. His distractions begin to take his mind away from day-to-day conversation. When his devoted wife

Elizabeth suggests they visit her mother for a weekend, the very thought brings an image of a lumbering hippopotamus to his mind. The next day, Elizabeth first notices something wrong when Reggie asks, "So, are we visiting the hippopotamus this weekend? Your mother . . . I just thought I'd call her a hippopotamus for a change." Such talk is just not like Reggie, who is fortunate to have a wife as forgiving as Elizabeth.

Reginald Perrin is presented in serial form, one of the first British comedy series to do so, which allows for the storyline and characters to evolve steadily and swiftly. The day finally comes when Reggie just can't take it anymore. He abandons the life he has known, leaving Sunshine Desserts and Elizabeth, and fakes his own death. But he reappears in disguise and with a new name, and wanders aimlessly and carefree. Loneliness sets in, however, and he eventually reunites with Elizabeth and opens an innovative store called Grot. Each item for sale in the Grot shop is very expensive, totally useless, and of little practical value to anyone, just as Reggie had intended. Among his inventory are such items as triangular-shaped Hula Hoops, non-stick glue, and bottomless ashtrays.

Much to Reggie's surprise, Grot becomes staggeringly popular, especially with those customers who want to find truly offensive gifts for people they hate. Before long Reggie finds himself at the helm of the Grot empire. When Sunshine Desserts goes bust, he hires his old colleagues, including his former boss, C. J. Reggie takes delight in wielding the same power over C. J. that he once had to heed on the opposite side of the executive desk. "There's just a vague possibility I might be able to offer you a job," he murmurs on the phone to C. J. "When will it be convenient for you to come in to see me? . . . Tuesday the first at 10:00? Fine, make it Friday the fourth at 3:00. Bye!"

Finding himself in the same routine he had previously escaped, Reggie gives up Grot and hits upon the inspiration to form a suburban commune with his employees. They set up their utopia in a house on a quiet street, where most of the members must sleep in backyard pup tents. Reggie is confident and enthusiastic about his new venture. He holds training sessions for his staff in the months before opening. All are assigned different duties

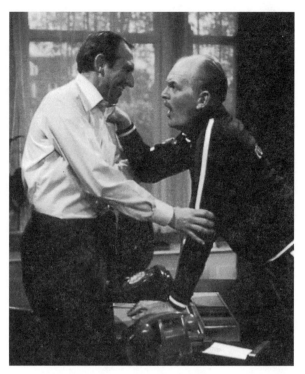

The tables have turned: Reggie, as founder of his own suburban commune, pacifies former boss C. J. (John Barron), who is having trouble adjusting to a new, spartan lifestyle.
BBC Worldwide

each day. C. J. is less than happy with his role as babysitter. At one point he storms into a meeting, extracts a Kermit the Frog doll out of his pants and scowls, "I didn't get where I am today by having green frogs thrust down my trousers!" Reggie, meanwhile, finds a professional cook named MacBlane, who is not only vaguely menacing, but whose thick Scottish accent makes him totally unintelligible.

The neighbors make their displeasure known when they stop by to complain about too much noise and too many cars and tents on the property. The proudly arrogant Reggie informs them that not only will hundreds more be arriving soon, but he resents petty complaints about parking and has no intention of doing anything about it. In fact, his new plan is to buy more houses on the street and expand the commune. How? In a comically cynical sequence, he has the others go house-to-house made up as Indian immigrants to greet the neighbors and state their intentions of moving into the neighborhood. (C. J. mistakenly dons black minstrel makeup and declares to one neighbor, "I didn't get where I is today without recognizing a mighty fine resident when I sees one.") Almost immediately, several homes on the street are up for sale.

Opening day finally arrives, but Reggie has only one booking, a lonely undertaker named Mr. Babbacombe. Embarrassed by the low turnout, Reggie devises a quick plan to disguise some of the staff as fellow guests. But it fails dismally, and Mr. Babbacombe leaves in a hurry. Reggie's utopia, however blissful on paper, hasn't quite measured up in practice. But his fortunes are destined to fall and rise for years to come.

Leonard Rossiter's schedule at that time had him working on *Reginald Perrin* about four months out of the year, usually in the summer. He would then return to Yorkshire in late winter or early spring to resume *Rising Damp*. The producer of *Reginald Perrin*, Gareth Gwenlan, remembers Leonard Rossiter's famous no-nonsense approach to his work. "He was a perfectionist," said Gwenlan, "He was an amazingly talented and very intense actor, and it wasn't so much that he didn't suffer fools gladly, he didn't suffer them at all . . . He was always professional, he always knew his words, and he was, 99 percent of the time, right in any instinct he had. And everyone else had to run to keep up with his speed."

Leonard Rossiter took on several roles for both TV and film in the late 1970s. In addition to *Rising Damp* and *Reginald Perrin*, he starred as a seedy wrestling manager in a six-episode comedy called *The Losers*. He also appeared with Peter Sellers in the feature film *The Pink Panther Strikes Again*. As mentioned earlier, Rossiter was starring in the series *Tripper's Day* in November 1984 when he died suddenly and, of course, far too early.

"[*Reginald Perrin*] was an extraordinary series to work on," said Gwenlan, "and he was an extraordinary man to work with."

BLESS ME, FATHER

LWT
1978-1981
18 Episodes

Written by Peter De Rosa
Produced by David Askey

Available on home video in the U.S.

Cast:

FATHER DUDDLESWELL	Arthur Lowe
FATHER NEIL BOYD	Daniel Abineri
MRS. PRING	Gabrielle Daye

Sitcoms centering on the lives of the clergy have been a staple on British television for decades. *Bless Me, Father* preceded several popular contemporary comedies (*All in Good Faith, Father Ted, The Vicar of Dibley*) featuring vicars as the lead characters.

By mining often unexpected comedy from its setting and characters, *Bless Me, Father* is a frequently hilarious series, benefiting not only by having Arthur Lowe as its star (he began this program shortly after completing his nine-year stint in *Dad's Army*), but also by having a former priest, Peter De Rosa, as its creator and sole writer. De Rosa had written a series of books under the pen name Neil Boyd, and based his sitcom on those stories.

Bless Me, Father takes place at the Parish of St. Jude in 1950-51. The series opens with crusty Father Duddleswell taking on his new young curate Father Neil. While respectful of his mentor, Father Neil is prone to rather cheeky remarks as he attempts to throw a bit of levity on Duddleswell's often somber demeanor. They're both attended to by the matronly housekeeper Mrs. Pring, who has known Father Duddleswell and his foibles for so long that any degree of reverence has long since fallen by the wayside. "He's really a very nice man until you get to know him," she explains to Father Neil. When the young curate expresses nervousness

about hearing his first confessions, Duddleswell tells Mrs. Pring, "He's probably expecting you to come along and unload your heinous sins!"

A typical story opens with Father Duddleswell supposedly treating Father Neil to a movie matinee, although the elder priest has conveniently forgotten his wallet. Once inside, Duddleswell's mocking of *The Bells of St. Mary's* is interrupted by a message on the public address system. He is late in performing a wedding ceremony back at the parish. A flat tire on his car in the theater parking lot adds to the delay. He phones ahead and tells Mrs. Pring to have the wedding party hold reception first and then he'll conduct the ceremony.

Once back at the parish, Father Neil stalls for his mentor and haltingly apologizes to the bridal couple and their guests, assuring them that while Father Duddleswell was involved in a mishap, he hasn't been hurt. Just then, a disheveled Duddleswell enters the hall with a smudged face and his arm in a sling. He plays the pity angle, but shortly afterward performs the ceremony without a hitch. He must then perform the civil ceremony in his office before the couple can be on their way.

Later, with the chaotic day apparently behind them, Duddleswell realizes that he performed the civil ceremony after 6:00 P.M., which is outside the legal parameters. The couple isn't married in the eyes of the law. Determined to put things right the next morning, he brings Father Neil with him to the hotel where the honeymoon has already commenced. They awkwardly visit the couple in their room (where they haven't left their bed yet) to tell them the news, and that they must perform the civil ceremony again. The husband is baffled. "Are you in the habit of sending bridal couples away from your church unmarried?" he demands. Father Neil can only reply sheepishly, "Very, very seldom."

BUTTERFLIES

BBC
1978–1982
28 Episodes

Written by Carla Lane
Produced and directed by Gareth Gwenlan,
Sydney Lotterby

Cast:

RIA PARKINSON	Wendy Craig
BEN PARKINSON	Geoffrey Palmer
ADAM	Nicholas Lyndhurst
RUSSELL	Andrew Hall
LEONARD	Bruce Montague
RUBY	Joyce Windsor
THOMAS	Michael Ripper

The Parkinson Family: (*left to right*) Russell (Andrew Hall), Ben (Geoffrey Palmer), Ria (Wendy Craig), and Adam (Nicholas Lyndhurst).
BBC Worldwide

Butterflies takes us into the life and mind of Ria Parkinson, an attractive housewife in her mid-forties going through a mid-life crisis. She is unquestionably devoted to her family, yet feels a gaping hole in her life that she can't identify. Her husband Ben is a successful dentist, her two teenage sons Russell and Adam tend to find trouble for themselves but are essentially good-natured, and they live in a comfortable suburban home. Ria, chronically introspective and prey to her own wistful musings on the meaning of life, feels the need to shake things up for herself.

Things get shaken considerably when Ria meets a man named Leonard in a restaurant one day. Leonard is a handsome, charming, and successful businessman who is also unhappily married and indeed separated from his wife. He has already begun playing the field but tends to feel sorry for himself for not having found true love in his life.

His driving offenses have also cost him his license for a year, and he must rely on his droll chauffeur Thomas to get around. Leonard makes no bones about his attraction to Ria, and she in turn finds herself attracted to his self-deprecating manner. Before they know it they've begun a clandestine affair—ostensibly platonic, but the growing sexual tension between them often has Ria agonizing over how to proceed.

Butterflies tackles this issue of adultery as well as other highly-charged topics (at one point Russell gets his girlfriend pregnant) with considerable humor and clever dialogue, and most episodes even include a bit of slapstick. However, creator/writer Carla Lane's philosophy seems to teeter on the edge of condoning adultery, for women anyway. Her scripts for *Butterflies* and her subsequent series *Solo* (starring Felicity Kendal) aren't quite as easy on the adulterous men of the world. However, Lane deserves credit for fleshing out her characters and making Ria truly torn about her feelings both for her husband and for Leonard.

Butterflies has been criticized, with some justification, for its somewhat melancholy tone overall. Ria's perpetual angst and endless introspection can leave the viewer confused whenever big laughs suddenly give way to her woe-is-me demeanor. Perhaps the series might be better described as a comedy-drama instead of a sitcom. For those who prefer their sitcoms to be more multi-dimensional (and even existential) than the majority of television offerings, *Butterflies* in its best moments proves a truly intriguing work.

Like many of her sitcom-writing peers, Carla Lane believes that even a successful television program should quit while it's ahead. After twenty-eight episodes, she determined that *Butterflies* had run its course. As is the case with the more established television writers in Britain, Lane's decision to end the series was the final word on the subject. "In England they don't press you to go on," she

said in a magazine interview. "You [Americans] think in terms of hundreds [of episodes]. I think in terms of how can that story be told well." When she was invited to Hollywood to discuss developing an American version of *Butterflies*, she soon fled back to England, appalled by the ideas American television executives offered her that, in Lane's opinion, would have cannibalized her heartfelt work.

Butterflies star Wendy Craig has also co-starred in *Brighton Belles*, an unsuccessful attempt to adapt *The Golden Girls* to the British way of life. Nicholas Lyndhurst and Geoffrey Palmer have both become fixtures in British sitcoms since *Butterflies*. Lyndhurst has starred in *Only Fools and Horses, The Two of Us, The Piglet Files*, and *Goodnight Sweetheart*. Geoffrey Palmer can be seen in an earlier, recurring role as Reginald Perrin's vague-minded brother-in-law, Jimmy. Other Britcoms in which Palmer has starred include *A Fairly Secret Army, Executive Stress, Hot Metal*, and *As Time Goes By*.

SHELLEY

Thames
1979-1992

Written by Peter Tilbury
Produced by Anthony Parker

Cast:

JAMES SHELLEY . . . . Hywel Bennett
FRAN SMITH . . . . Belinda Sinclair
MRS. HAWKINS . . . . Josephine Tewson

> The jaunty theme music for
> *Shelley* was written by the
> late Ron Grainer, who also
> wrote the memorable themes
> for *The Avengers* and *The
> Prisoner*.

Shelley follows the exploits of James Shelley, an intelligent young man with a degree in geography that has been of decidedly little use in his efforts to find employment. In truth, however, Shelley's search for a job rarely has him expending any more energy than is absolutely necessary. His girlfriend (and eventual wife) Fran tries to be patient while waiting for a breakthrough of some sort for Shelley's career, but she regularly expresses her disdain for his laziness. Whenever the subject of his chronic unemployment arises, Shelley tends to change the subject or deflect the blame by waxing philosophical about anything and everything, and to anyone within earshot.

Writer Peter Tilbury created *Shelley* at a time when unemployment in Britain had reached record proportions in the 1970s. "I knew what it was like to be unemployed," he said. "And at that time unemployment was a big deal over here. It has remained so, but we first found the magic figure of one million people unemployed . . . at that time it was a very traumatic figure." He didn't see unemployment dealt with realistically in TV situation comedy. The effort to correct that flaw gave him the impetus to create *Shelley*. "Once you've started, all you've got to do is keep turning out the episodes, which is the hard part," he said.

Shelley enjoyed a long and successful, if somewhat erratic run. Shortly after the first four episodes were aired, ITV went on strike and the remaining episodes didn't air until the following year.

The second series sees Shelley and Fran getting married and Fran getting pregnant. Most episodes devote long scenes to conversations in their humble flat. In one scene, Fran gets depressed watching the news on one channel, and hopes the BBC news might be more cheerful. "You're clutching at straws, Fran," replies Shelley with his typical know-it-all demeanor. "The BBC's charter specifically forbids cheerfulness. They've got an alarm at TV Centre that goes off the minute an optimist walks into the building."

Shelley continues to find and lose jobs along the way, and at one point lands a position as a copywriter for an advertising agency. Fran's objection to his ads for cigarette companies, however, sounds the death knell for his tenure there.

In the third series (written by veteran writers Andy Hamilton and Colin Bostock-Smith), Fran gives birth to their daughter Emma, but loses her patience waiting for Shelley to become a good provider for the family. She eventually leaves him to wallow in his misery.

The end of the series' initial run in 1983 had Shelley moving to the United States, but he returned in 1988, with the series called *The Return of Shelley*. Still more episodes were later produced under the original *Shelley* title. The television series ended for good in September of 1990 with Shelley moving into a community of elderly people. However, the BBC later produced a radio version of the series, for which Peter Tilbury re-wrote his older scripts.

Josephine Tewson, who plays Shelley's nosy landlady Mrs. Hawkins, would reappear on *Keeping up Appearances* as Liz, Hyacinth Bucket's nervous neighbor.

TO THE MANOR BORN

BBC
1979–1981
21 Episodes

Written by Peter Spence
Produced by Gareth Gwenlan

Available on home video in the U.S.

Cast:

AUDREY FFORBES-HAMILTON	Penelope Keith
RICHARD DEVERE	Peter Bowles
MARJORY FROBISHER	Angela Thorne
MRS. POLOUVICKA	Daphne Heard
BRABINGER	John Rudling
RECTOR	Gerald Sim

Audrey (Penelope Keith) is now a guest in what used to be her own home, and it doesn't sit well with her! Richard DeVere (Peter Bowles) is the new owner of Grantleigh Manor. *BBC Worldwide*

To the Manor Born is a decidedly British series, with a setting and storyline that may not be very identifiable for some Americans. However, there's no effort needed to enjoy the rocky relationship that eventually blooms between aristocratic snob Audrey fforbes-Hamilton and self-made man Richard DeVere.

Creator/writer Peter Spence was a sketch writer at the BBC when he heard of plans to develop a series for Penelope Keith, who had gained great popularity as Margo on the sitcom *Good Neighbors*. He wondered what it would be like if the haughty Margo really were the blue-blooded English aristocrat she aspired to be. Spence came up with a character and storyline he felt were suitable for Keith's talents. He was proven right beyond his wildest expectations.

To the Manor Born was originally intended to be a radio series. A single pilot episode was recorded but never broadcast, when it was decided that television would be the better medium for the program.

As the series opens, Audrey is attending the funeral of her not-so-dear-departed husband just beyond the grounds of their estate, Grantleigh Manor. Rather than mourning her loss like a good widow should, she shocks her friend Marjory on their walk home by finding a secluded spot to jump for joy. Her beloved home has been in the fforbes-Hamilton family for 400 years, and now she has it all to herself.

Audrey's bliss doesn't last long, however. Shortly after returning home, she is informed that her late husband has left behind a mountain of debt. In fact, says her advisor, the debt is so vast that the only way Audrey can crawl out from under it is to sell Grantleigh Manor. Stunned and heartbroken, she puts the estate up for auction, hoping to make the highest bid with the money she has left. But her plan is foiled when she is outbid by the suave Richard DeVere, founder and owner of a supermarket empire. Audrey's life has changed radically in a matter of minutes. All she has left is her new residence down the drive at the estate lodge, a fraction of the size of Grantleigh Manor. Full of resentment, she can comfort herself only by thinking of the new owner as a temporary "caretaker" until she somehow wins back her beloved home. Still, she can't help but to find herself somewhat attracted to the new lord of the manor.

Richard DeVere is both more and less than what he presents to the world. His real name is Bedrich Polouvicka, the son of Czechoslovakian immigrants. His Anglicized name is just part of his overall strategy for climbing the ladder of success, which he has thus far done with great skill. But his mother, who insists on calling him Bedrich, has moved into Grantleigh Manor with him, and shrewdly takes advantage of this by needling him about his awkward and sometimes crass nouveau riche ways. More importantly, she is convinced that Richard and Audrey belong together on a permanent basis, and encourages their unsteady romance at every opportunity.

Now that Audrey has been relegated to life in the lodge, she finds her pride tested on a regular basis, especially in her social circles. In one episode, Richard's mother has convinced him to throw a party at the manor. His snobbish guests, however, not only trade gossip about his supposedly shady business practices, but also remark to Audrey about her pale complexion and need of a vacation. Unable to afford her accustomed holiday, she sets about leading everyone to believe she'll be away for two weeks, but actually hides in the lodge under a sun lamp, listening to Spanish language instruction records. Richard, out on a stroll one day, catches a glimpse of Audrey under the sun lamp. When she "returns" from her trip, she throws a party for herself and convinces her guests of her wonderful time in Spain. Richard takes her aside and informs her that he knows of her deception. Seeing her social life flash before her eyes, Audrey agrees to stop spreading false rumors about his business (although she considers her comments innocuous). In return, Richard agrees to keep mum about Audrey's exotic vacation in her own living room.

The basic format of many episodes begins with the reluctant lovebirds getting along reasonably well at first, only to have Richard commit some sort of heinous act (from Audrey's perspective) that causes war to break out between them again. Once resolved, a sudden twist of the tale at the end of the episode sets them feuding once more.

An example of this is an episode in which Audrey, as Girl Scout county commissioner, hears of Richard's reluctance to sponsor the Grantleigh Boy Scout troop. The boys will be building and racing their raft down the river, hoping to collect enough money to build a new scout hut. Richard is actually planning to donate a hut, but keeps that fact to himself at first. Audrey confronts him to lecture him about his petty attitude. He cuts her off, telling her how he resents her constant criticisms of how he is running the manor. He adds, with characteristic smugness, "Why do you keep finding fault? I'll tell you why. Firstly, because you want to prove to everybody that you're still Dame High-and-Mighty around here, and secondly, you rather enjoy coming over here to see me." They manage to put aside their bickering in favor of plans for a picnic that weekend.

Audrey and Richard stand before Audrey's beloved Grantleigh Manor. *BBC Worldwide*

Richard pulls out all the stops to present Audrey with an idyllic country picnic: full table service by the river, a parasol for her, a straw hat for him, and other old-fashioned, romantic touches. She loves it, and accompanies him to a waiting gondola at the riverbank. Just then a prop man interrupts to tell Richard the props will have to be returned soon. The entire setup is actually a promotion for one of Richard's salad cream products. An incensed Audrey sends Richard adrift in the boat, where he collides with the Boy Scout raft and plunges into the water. Their relationship has come full circle once again.

"But then we were told we've got to get these people together a bit now," said Peter Spence, "because it's what the audience expects. I never really believed in the romantic aspects of it . . . I found it hard to write it as a real romance, but that's because I'm a comedy writer and don't write real romance very well. So I was shy of that because I didn't quite have the vocabulary for it, and was slightly out of my depth. . . . There was a growing affection [between them], but that was more on his terms than hers. I think he was quite amused by her. He stood slightly aloof from it all and let her have her little whims in a quite generous and affectionate way."

Despite Spence's skittish approach to the couple's romance, their fate was pretty much inevitable. In the program's final episode (written by Christopher Bond), Richard breaks the news to Audrey that a bit of misfortune has left his financial status floundering. He has no choice but to sell Grantleigh for some quick cash. She can relate to his dilemma and feels sorry for him. But within a day or two, she learns that she is the main beneficiary of a wealthy uncle who has just passed away. She later chats with Richard's mother, who is packing to move back to London with him. They discuss Audrey and Richard's lost opportunity to marry. "Why didn't it happen?" asks Mrs. Polouvicka. "He never asked me," replies Audrey matter-of-factly. But she adds that she wouldn't have accepted his proposal as long as he owned the manor anyway, for fear that he'd misinterpret her motives.

At the auction, Audrey has Brabinger bid quietly but aggressively on her behalf. It works. She regains ownership, moves back in, and

promptly throws a party. During a moonlit walk with Richard, he mentions his inclination to chuck his business altogether. She responds by surprising him with the suggestion that he marry her. Now that external factors have fallen into place, true love finally has its chance to blossom unencumbered. And so it does.

While following the relationship between Audrey and Richard, *To the Manor Born* at the same time satirizes the British class system and how many of the traditional manors in the late 1970s and early 1980s were brought up by people who didn't belong to the old feudal class system. "It was about the war between old and new," Peter Spence said, "between the new money and the old class system." Spence has more than a few personal connections with the setting of *To the Manor Born*:

> I myself lived in the place where we filmed it. That is in fact the home of my wife's family. I lived on a farm next door to that. This is in Somerset, in the West country. They had that house and a thousand-acre estate which they farmed, and ran a sort of wildlife park there as well. And I lived there for about three years just after I was married, on a neighboring farm. And I supposed I soaked up the country life while I was there, although I'm a town person myself. And I obviously registered certain types of people and certain attitudes, and read into that.

Peter Bowles knew he did the right thing when he went against his agent's initial advice to turn down the series. Bowles had been starring in *Rumpole of the Bailey* when he was offered a new sitcom with Penelope Keith. Having already turned down the chance to work with her in *Good Neighbors*, he was determined to read the scripts for *To the Manor Born*. "I read the scripts and thought I've got to do this, somehow or other," he said. He personally phoned the heads of both BBC Comedy and ITV Comedy (which produced *Rumpole*) and persuaded them to meet and arrange rehearsal rooms so he could rehearse one show in the morning and the other in the afternoon. "I knew that *To the Manor Born* was recorded on a Sunday, and I recorded *Rumpole* on Thursdays.

That's how I managed to do both of them . . . and the extraordinary thing was that I was appearing in a play as well at this time."

To the Manor Born achieved near-record ratings by the end of its first series. By the last episode of that series in November of 1979, almost twenty-four million viewers were following the love-hate relationship between Audrey and Richard. Both this episode and another from November of 1980 still rank among the top-rated programs of all time in Britain. All who were involved with the show were stunned by its popularity with the viewing public. Fans of both Penelope Keith and Peter Bowles were later treated to a reunion of sorts when Bowles took over the role of Donald Fairchild opposite Keith in the Thames TV series *Executive Stress*.

In 1997, *To the Manor Born* was reincarnated for radio, its original home. Peter Spence adapted six of his old television scripts and wrote four new episodes for the series. Penelope Keith and Angela Thorne reprised their roles as Audrey and Marjory, with Keith Barron assuming the role as Richard. Keith said at the time that playing Audrey once again was like "slipping on a nice, comfy pair of gloves."

PART II

"Listen very carefully, I shall say this only once..." Britcoms of the 1980s

BRITISH TV IN THE 1980S

In November of 1982, Channel Four Television was born, as a wholly-owned subsidiary of the IBA (Independent Broadcasting Authority, formerly the ITA). As intended, Channel Four's programming soon earned a reputation as being experimental, innovative, sometimes controversial, and appealing to younger audiences (the original *Max Headroom* was a Channel Four program). It was in this energetic climate that a new wave of "alternative comedians" took the world of British television comedy by storm. Comedian/writer Ben Elton and the cast of Elton's surreal, live-action cartoon series, *The Young Ones* (Adrian Edmondson, Rik Mayall, Nigel Planer, and Christopher Ryan) led the way in filling the vacuum left by the legendary Monty Python troupe. Other comedians included in this post-Python alternative group were the stars of the 1979 hit, *Not the Nine O'Clock News*: Rowan Atkinson, Pamela Stephenson, Mel Smith, and

Griff Rhys-Jones. Atkinson, of course, is better known for *The Black Adder* and *Mr. Bean*. Mel Smith and Griff Rhys-Jones starred in their own sketch series *Alas Smith and Jones*. Dawn French and Jennifer Saunders translated their stage improvisation success into their own sketch series. Other alternative comedians include the anarchic Alexei Sayle (*Alexei Sayle's Stuff*) and Lenny Henry (*Chef!*). All of these extremely creative, funny, and versatile performers have appeared on television and on stage together in various combinations, such as in the popular *Secret Policeman's Ball* and the *Comic Relief* series of charity shows. Their camaraderie has even resulted in the marriage of Dawn French to Lenny Henry and of Jennifer Saunders to Adrian Edmondson.

Comedy writer Eric Chappell (*Rising Damp, The Bounder*), who might be considered part of the older, more conventional school of sitcom writers, assessed the rise of the alternative comedians:

> I think what happened was—of course the producers get younger, they come from that generation, they're impressed more by what was considered to be the university set that provides this sort of anarchic comedy . . . and they feel they've got to be up-to-date themselves, so they commission these people. And of course the people themselves are often performers, so you're getting two for the price of one, a writer and a performer. Also, they tend to work in a bunch so they commission each other. They're all friends, they all dine together . . . I don't

complain, what they do often is very, very good. What I'm saying is there's room for all of us, really.

Elsewhere in the world of British television, both the BBC and Channel Four inaugurated breakfast time programming in 1983. The programs were, and still are, not unlike America's *Today Show* and *Good Morning, America*. (It should be noted that 1983 was rather a late start for a concept with which Americans have been familiar for decades.) Over thirty production companies applied to produce Channel Four's breakfast program, the winner being *The Big Breakfast*, co-produced by Planet 24 (of which Bob Geldof was a company director).

Then came media titan Rupert Murdoch and his Sky Broadcasting, a satellite-to-home service available to those who had the foresight (and money) to buy a satellite dish. Sky Channel, the first commercial satellite channel, became available in January of 1984, offering four channels. The only notable competitor at the time was British Satellite Broadcasting (a consortium including, among others, Granada TV and the Virgin Group), which aimed higher, so to speak, by using a more powerful satellite than Murdoch's. BSB also offered five channels and a smaller receiver that could be hung out a window, as opposed to the larger dish required for Sky Channel. Despite these promising features and considerable encouragement from large regional broadcasters in Britain, British Satellite Broadcasting ran into technological snags and delays that allowed Murdoch to strengthen his position.

Hi-De-Hi

BBC
1980-1988
70 Episodes

Written by Jimmy Perry and David Croft
Produced by David Croft

Available on home video in the U.S.

Cast:

Jeffrey Fairbrother	Simon Cadell
Gladys Pugh	Ruth Madoc
Ted Bovis	Paul Shane
Spike	Jeffrey Holland
Peggy	Su Pollard
Barry	Barry Howard
Yvonne	Diane Holland
Partridge	Leslie Dwyer
Fred	Felix Bowness

Jeffrey Fairbrother (Simon Cadell, *seated center*), surrounded by the Maplin's Resort staff. *BBC Worldwide*

This long-running series is a typical example of producer David Croft's penchant for creating a large cast of colorful characters who specialize in getting each other in and out of trouble each week. The setting is Maplin's Holiday Camp, circa 1959. The resort is owned by Joe Maplin, who remains unseen throughout the series but makes his presence known via phone calls and grammatically crude letters. The daily responsibilities of running the camp's entertainment fall upon the amiable but uptight Jeffrey Fairbrother, whose low threshold for embarrassment makes him a questionable choice to preside over the eccentric Maplin entertainment staff. Jeffrey's assistant, Gladys Pugh, finds him irresistibly desirable despite his reserved personality and is forever hinting that they should explore the more personal side of their relationship. The camp's rotund host and comedian Ted Bovis is the usual instigator of schemes among the staff. The others include Spike, Ted's apprentice comedian; Peggy, the clumsy but earnest chambermaid who yearns to

become an official Yellowcoat assistant someday; Barry and Yvonne, the snooty ballroom dancers whose glory days are long gone; and Mr. Partridge, the camp's crabby old Punch and Judy puppeteer who hates children.

David Croft laments that the series' setting may have been a bit obscure for viewers who aren't familiar with the concept of holiday camps. "I think we've suffered from that because although it's a funny show, you don't necessarily know what it's about," he said. A real holiday camp in Clacton, Essex, was used for the location scenes.

Croft later recruited Paul Shane, Jeffrey Holland, and Su Pollard from *Hi-De-Hi* to star in the comedy series *You Rang, M'Lord?*, a satire of the classic drama *Upstairs, Downstairs*.

Tragically, *Hi-De-Hi* star Simon Cadell, who had become David Croft's son-in-law, died in March of 1996 after a long struggle with cancer. He was only forty-five, but had already earned the praise of his peers with his comic and dramatic roles on television as well as in the theater.

Yes, Minister/Yes, Prime Minister

BBC-2
Yes, Minister
1980-1984
22 Episodes
Yes, Prime Minister
1986-1987
16 Episodes

Written by Antony Jay and Jonathan Lynn
Directed and produced by Sydney Lotterby
(first series), Peter Whitmore

Available on home video in the U.S.

Cast

Rt. Hon. James Hacker . . . . Paul Eddington
Sir Humphrey Appleby . . . . . . Nigel Hawthorne
Bernard Woolley . . . . Derek Fowlds
Annie Hacker . . . . Diana Hoddinott

The perpetually befuddled Jim Hacker (Paul Eddington, *center*) with his masters of dubious doubletalk, Sir Humphrey (Nigel Hawthorne) and Bernard Woolley (Derek Fowlds). *BBC Worldwide*

It is probably safe to say that no sitcom, British or American, has ever achieved the level of literacy and sophistication of *Yes, Minister*, one of the most admired Britcoms of the 1980s. While audiences in the U.S. seem to have little interest in television comedies set snugly in the world of American government and politics, our British counterparts embraced *Yes, Minister* and even supported its evolution into *Yes, Prime Minister* for two more series. It is that rarest of programs that requires more than a modicum of intelligence to follow, and then rewards the viewer with funny, sharply drawn characters and deft political satire. Margaret Thatcher, Britain's Prime Minister at the time of the show's run, was known to be a big fan, as were many Parliament members and other high-ranking government officials.

The first series opens as James Hacker begins his term as the newly elected Minister of Administrative Affairs (a title created by the writers). The new position gives him the responsibility of insuring that government policies are formulated and carried out with a minimum of red tape. He is eager to change the system for the better, yet he's a little naive about how things really get done in government.

Enter Sir Humphrey Appleby, Permanent Under-Secretary. Before our fresh-faced Minister can get comfortable in his new leather chair, Hacker meets his philosophical nemesis. Humphrey thrives on maintaining the status quo, proudly revels in red tape, and is determined to foil Hacker's attempts to achieve true progress on just about any issue. He is a master of double-talk and gobbledygook, and when need be, can effortlessly create a verbal labyrinth leaving Hacker dizzy with confusion.

The man caught in the middle of this battle of wills is Hacker's private secretary, Bernard

Woolley, whose allegiance to the Minister is routinely tested by Humphrey's persuasive manner. Bernard wants only to do the right thing, but is sometimes unsure of what the right thing is. Still, he is an invaluable presence to Hacker except when he volunteers to explain a fine point of government bureaucracy. Bernard's gift for lapsing into gibbering double-talk is equal to Humphrey's.

Yes, Minister grew from an idea by Antony Jay, a longtime producer of public affairs programs who had acquired considerable knowledge of politicians and the workings of government. After mulling over the comic possibilities of a show about the tug-of-war relationship between a Cabinet Minister and his Permanent Secretary, he approached veteran comedy writer Jonathan Lynn, who loved the idea. The two of them submitted a script to the BBC in 1977, but the cautious fellows at the Comedy Department preferred to wait until after the General Election. Finally in February of 1980, *Yes, Minister* made its successful debut.

Any episode of *Yes, Minister* clearly illustrates how different a series it is from American sitcoms. The fact that it takes place at the highest levels of government and treats current issues with considerable authenticity is impressive. Writers Lynn and Jay received help from confidential sources near or at the top which ensured a realistic portrayal of how the British government really operates behind the scenes. Even producer Peter Whitmore never knew the identity of the sources. "I make a great point of not trying to know," he said during the show's production, "because if I start treating it as a documentary we might lose our way. We have got to remember we are there to make people laugh. It is basically a comedy."

Another feature that distinguishes *Yes, Minister* from other sitcoms is the heavily verbal nature of each episode. The dialogue moves at a brisk pace and requires viewers to pay attention, especially when rather complicated issues are discussed. One episode in particular, "Equal Opportunities," includes a scene in which Jim Hacker and Humphrey talk from their respective sides of Hacker's desk for a full seven minutes. Such an extensive scene consisting of nothing but dialogue between two characters is a rarity in American situation comedy, but in the Minister's office the time flies thanks to the endearing charac-

ters, impeccable acting, and, of course, the fact that it is very funny.

Yes, Minister is not a claustrophobic marathon of highbrow dialogue. It is also a strongly visual show and has no snobbish objection to delighting in the occasional sight gag. Several of the finest episodes indeed venture out of the Minister's office, such as those featuring Hacker or Humphrey appearing on TV and radio talk shows which never go as smoothly as planned. Hacker's visit to a city farm in "The Quality of Life" obliges him to give a speech to an audience consisting mostly of children and small furry animals. It doesn't help matters when he pulls out the wrong speech from his pocket and begins with, "There is quite rightly an increasing concern about high-rise buildings. But I'm happy to be able to reassure all of you members of the Architectural Association. . . ." He suddenly realizes his error and frantically retrieves the proper speech from his coat pocket as the confused children wait in silence.

In "The Compassionate Society," Hacker tours a new, fully-staffed hospital complete with everything—except patients. At one point, he takes a look around a completely empty ward, then steps into a bustling administrative office. The look of bewilderment on his face says it all. As usual, he has Humphrey to thank for this stellar example of bureaucracy gone berserk. (Humphrey later defends the situation by saying, "You talk as if the staff has nothing to do simply because there are no patients there. . . . Those five hundred people are seriously overworked. The full establishment should be six hundred and fifty.")

A typical week in the life of producing *Yes, Minister* consisted of almost non-stop activity. Each Monday morning the actors would meet at the BBC rehearsal rooms in North Acton. The building, nicknamed the Acton Hilton, consists mostly of eighteen bleak, scantily-furnished rooms designed for rehearsals of comedies and dramas. Here the actors have their first read-through with the writers in attendance. They spend Tuesday learning their lines, rehearse without scripts on Wednesday, and meet with the writers again on Friday. The script is polished and refined all week. Rehearsals continue on Friday and Saturday at Acton and on Sunday at the BBC Television Centre. The show begins its taping before a studio audience at 8:00 P.M. on Sunday. The next morning the process begins all over again at Acton.

The first three series of *Yes, Minister* met with such praise that it became the first comedy series ever to win the BAFTA Best Comedy award three years in a row. Still, the creators were ready to take the series to an even higher level in several ways.

In December of 1985, *Yes, Minister* presented a special one-hour episode entitled "Party Games." In this transition episode, the Christmas season sees several major shakeups taking place in government. First, Cabinet Secretary Sir Arnold Robinson has retired—and who has been appointed to succeed him but none other than his good friend, Sir Humphrey Appleby. The Prime Minister also announces his plans to retire, but none of the likely candidates seem suitable for the job, at least according to the ever-scheming Humphrey and Arnold who need a prime minister with a fairly pliable mind.

Humphrey digs up mountains of scandalous dirt on the two strongest candidates, supplies Hacker with the information, and Hacker uses the information to dissuade them both from pursuing the top spot. Once he has shunted aside his roadblocks to Number Ten Downing Street, he needs some favorable publicity to boost his own popularity. He finds it in a nationally televised speech in which he takes a tough stand on a hopelessly trivial issue, the fate of the Eurosausage. It works though, and the next day he runs unopposed and is elected Party Leader.

As everything falls into place, Jim Hacker becomes the new Prime Minister. By his side are, as always, Sir Humphrey, who is now the new Cabinet Secretary, and Bernard, who has been asked to stay on as Private Secretary.

This finely plotted episode launches *Yes, Prime Minister*. With Jim Hacker and his cohorts now at Number Ten Downing Street, they are able to tackle even weightier matters than before, such as international diplomatic relations, arms sales, spying, and, as always, internal crises of all sorts. The series continues its political escapades without skipping a beat. If anything, the writing becomes even sharper as time goes on.

Although Humphrey's endless scheming usually leaves Jim Hacker befuddled, occasionally the tables are turned, especially if Hacker comes across a bit of information that could give cause for Humphrey to squirm.

Humphrey comes under the gun in "One of Us." Prime Minister Hacker learns that John Halstead, the former head of MI-5 (Britain's intelligence agency), had in fact passed on secrets to the Russians throughout his tenure in the 1960s. Halstead's confession was found in his papers after his death. He was once investigated by a committee when the press reported rumors of his spying activities. The chief inquisitor on that committee was Sir Humphrey, who had cleared Halstead but apparently missed many obvious questions. The present Director General of MI-5 suggests to Hacker that the gentle handling of Halstead may have been deliberate, possibly due to collusion. Hacker confronts Humphrey about it, and promptly sends him on "gardening leave" until the remaining papers are examined. Humphrey protests. "You can't check up on everything—you never know *what* you might find!" he argues in typical fashion. He consults with Sir Arnold, who later hands Hacker a diary entry by John Halstead. In it, Halstead thoroughly mocks Humphrey's incompetent questioning on the committee. Hacker takes great delight in reading the paper to the humiliated Humphrey, who is finally cleared of any potential suspicion but is left humbled by the report.

Despite the occasional Jim Hacker "victory" over Humphrey, most of the *Yes, Minister/Yes, Prime Minister* episodes gleefully place Hacker in a tight spot that requires one of Humphrey's devious solutions. Hacker is usually left to choose the lesser of two evils to solve the problem. Of course, his

The big move—our bureaucratic heroes inherit Number Ten Downing Street as Jim Hacker becomes Prime Minister. *BBC Worldwide*

Although *Yes, Minister* and *Yes, Prime Minister* were favorites of former British Prime Minister Margaret Thatcher, star Paul Eddington was not one to return the admiration. He was a staunch political liberal and strongly disapproved of Thatcher's conservative policies.

choice inevitably manages to benefit Humphrey's interests anyway, leaving the strange, symbiotic relationship between the two intact.

The creativity and care that went into *Yes, Minister/Yes, Prime Minister* didn't flag even when it came time to produce a book version of the series. Popular BBC programs, especially comedies, are often marketed in book form. Instead of presenting what would essentially amount to a short story version of each episode, Antony Jay and Jonathan Lynn devised *The Complete Yes, Minister* volumes, subtitled *The Diaries of a Cabinet Minister* (followed by a *Yes, Prime Minister* volume).

Each chapter is indeed adapted from the original episode, but in the form of Jim Hacker's diary, which Jay and Lynn have "edited." Mixed in with Jim Hacker's daily entries are excerpts of his famous exchanges with Humphrey and Bernard,

and copies of handwritten memos, letters, press releases, and documents all pertaining to the story. The approach is not only appropriate to the setting of the series, but considerably livelier than the short story form and makes it almost as much fun to read as it is to watch.

It should come as no surprise that the talented members of the cast continued their careers with further success. American audiences are most familiar with Nigel Hawthorne's Academy Award-nominated starring role in the film, *The Madness of King George*, which he had played earlier on the London stage. Derek Fowlds has been seen in the imported British drama *Heartbeat*, in which his role as a surly, intimidating police inspector seems light years away from his portrayal as the soft-spoken Bernard Woolley. Paul Eddington appeared onstage in 1992 in a revival of Harold Pinter's "No Man's Land," playing opposite Pinter. Eddington was nominated for an Olivier Award for his performance. In 1994, despite suffering from terminal cancer, he appeared in the West End production of "Home" with Richard Briers, his close friend and co-star twenty years earlier in *Good Neighbors*. Unfortunately, it was Eddington's last acting project. He died in November of 1995 at the age of sixty-eight.

ONLY FOOLS AND HORSES

BBC
1981-1993
61 Episodes,
13 Christmas Specials

Produced by Ray Butt, Gareth Gwenlan
Written by John Sullivan

Cast:

DEREK "DEL BOY" TROTTER .... David Jason
RODNEY .... Nicholas Lyndhurst
GRANDAD .... Lennard Pearce (1981-1983)
UNCLE ALBERT .... Buster Merryfield

(*Left to right*): Rodney (Nicholas Lyndhurst), Uncle Albert (Buster Merryfield), and master entrepreneur, Del Boy (David Jason). *BBC Worldwide*

Only Fools and Horses is another example of a popular and endearing sitcom which struck the fancy of British TV viewers and firmly secured a permanent place in their hearts. The series garnered historic ratings and has been one of the few programs in history to top the twenty million viewer mark. Make no mistake about it—this program is not merely loved in Britain, it is cherished.

Del Boy Trotter is a wheeler-dealer forever scheming to make his first million. His somewhat nebulous business, Trotter's Independent Trading Company, consists of little more than Del dealing out of his Robin Reliant (a three-wheeled car) in South London's Peckham market. Del somehow manages to regularly come across discarded products he feels are guaranteed to take Britain's consumers by storm. The only guarantee, however, is that his schemes will backfire and return him to square one. Del's philosophy is reflected in the show's theme song which claims, "Only fools and horses work."

Del lives in a council tower flat with his younger, naive brother Rodney and, in the earlier series, Grandad (Lennard Pearce played Grandad until his death in 1984). Buster Merryfield as Uncle Albert replaced him and stayed on for the remainder of the series' run. Del always manages to coerce the others to assist him in his schemes, countering their reluctance by conjuring up images of potential wealth.

"A Touch of Glass" opens with Del picking up a bulk supply of Korean-made porcelain cat music boxes. The cat revolves on a platter to the tune of "How Much Is That Doggie In The Window?". Rodney and Grandad are as skeptical about the future resale potential as Del is confident. Driving home through the countryside, they encounter a woman stuck on the side of the road with car trouble. She is Lady Richmere, whom Del gleefully agrees to tow back to her estate. Once invited inside by the Lordship, Del swaggers through the sitting room, admiring the various works of art and claiming to know a thing or two about them, but his common ways aren't fooling anyone, least of all the embarrassed Rodney and

Grandad. Del later hears the Lordship on the phone complaining about the fees involved for having the estate's authentic Louis XIV chandeliers cleaned and repaired. He meets the Lordship in the entrance hall, admires the chandeliers, and casually informs the Lordship about his family history as chandelier makers and renovation specialists. The Lordship promptly asks Del to do the job.

Back at the flat, Del tries to convince Rodney how the job could be their big break, and one he's had coming for a long time. "I deserve a bit of the good life," he reasons, "Worked hard enough for it. Where has it got me? Nowhere. We live half a mile up in the sky in this Lego set built by the council, we've got a three-wheeled van with a bald tire, we drink in wine bars where the only thing that's got a vintage is the governor's wife."

After convincing the others to help out, they arrive at the mansion ready for work. Grandad goes upstairs to remove the bolt holding up one of the chandeliers. Del and Rodney stretch out a blanket between them to catch it. Grandad loosens the bolt, but it's holding the *other* chandelier, twenty feet away. The fixture comes crashing to the floor as Del and Rodney stand motionless with their blanket outstretched. They all inspect the wreckage as the horrified butler arrives and says he's going to call the Lordship (who's away on his holiday) immediately. Del makes sure the Lordship doesn't have their address or phone number before racing the others out of the house and into the van for a quick but clumsy getaway.

Later in the series' run, both Del and Rodney find love. Rodney marries Cassandra, and Del marries Raquel. A fifty-minute special episode opens as Raquel is days away from having a baby. Del is over the moon about it, and has even attended pre-natal classes with her. Career-wise, he is also excited about having acquired a boxful of wigs that he intends to sell to "the tarts at the Nag's Head Pub." However, Rodney soon discovers that the box contains men's toupees instead. Uncle Albert sees no problem, citing that he's seen a lot of bald men coming out of one particular building on Arnold Road. "That's the Hare Krishna temple!" Del explains. Rodney meanwhile is having marriage problems with Cassandra, and the two have sepa-

rated. Discouraged, he tells Uncle Albert, "If there is such a thing as reincarnation, knowing my luck I'll come back as me." Luckily Cassandra is willing to try to talk things out. Not only do the two talk, but they also end up in bed together.

When Raquel's labor pains begin, Del and Albert take her to the hospital. Del phones Rodney at Cassandra's flat, and, despite her fib that Rodney isn't with her, tells her to get Rodney out of her bed and send him to the hospital. After what seems like hours of screaming, Raquel finally delivers a son. In a quiet moment, the family gathers in her room where Del takes the baby to the window to give him his first glimpse of the world. Speaking softly in his Cockney accent, the beaming father tells his new son, "I've wanted to do things and be someone, but I never had what it took. You're different. You're gonna live my dreams for me, and do all the things I've wanted to do, and you're gonna come back and tell me about them. . . . I've mucked about all my life, and I never knew the reason until now. This is what it's all about. I was born for this moment." The warmth and eloquence of Del's words serve as a special gift from series creator/ writer John Sullivan to his millions of loyal fans. No doubt there wasn't a dry eye in the country.

Sullivan has been one of British television's impressively prolific sitcom writers of the past two decades. His other credits include *Citizen Smith* (starring Robert Lindsay, the original star of the Broadway hit *Me and My Gal*), and *Dear John*, which was later adapted in the U.S. and starred Judd Hirsch.

Despite his lengthy list of television successes, John Sullivan's funny and heartwarming scripts for *Only Fools and Horses* will no doubt stand as his most appreciated gift to the annals of British television comedy.

Gorden Kaye (star of *'Allo, 'Allo!*): "It's the sort of show that if there's a new one on, or a new series on, the streets are deserted . . . theaters have got nobody coming because it's the first night of *Only Fools and Horses*. So it's got that kind of clout."

THE BOUNDER

Yorkshire Television
1982-1983
14 Episodes

Written by Eric Chappell
Produced by Vernon Lawrence

Cast:

HOWARD BOOTH .... Peter Bowles
TREVOR MOUNTJOY .... George Cole
MARY MOUNTJOY .... Rosalind Ayres
LAURA .... Isla Blair

Howard (Peter Bowles) thinks fast to convince Mary (Rosalind Ayres) and Trevor (George Cole) that he has a smashing anniversary celebration planned for them.
Yorkshire Television

The Bounder is a cleverly amusing and popular series that provides Peter Bowles (*To The Manor Born*) with yet another suave, smooth-talking character to play. It was also the third successful series for creator/writer Eric Chappell, who wrote *Only When I Laugh* (also featuring Bowles) and *Rising Damp*, starring Leonard Rossiter.

Peter Bowles had done three series of *Only When I Laugh* and was asked to do a fourth. "And I said to my agent, 'Would you say that I'd only do a fourth if they'd give me my own series?' And he said, 'Oh I can't possibly do that, it's so cheeky.' And I said, 'Well, try it.' And he tried it, and they said, 'Yes, all right, has he got any ideas?' So I went along with some ideas, and between Eric and I . . . we came up with this Bounder idea. Nothing ventured, nothing gained . . ." Eric Chappell wasn't bothered by Bowles's proposition. "I was happy to

do it," he said, "because I had got an idea. I thought he could play the bounder, a confidence trickster-type cad. And so that's what I did. It was no problem. So we had him for the fourth series [of *Only When I Laugh*] and he had a series of his own!"

As a con man recently released from prison for embezzlement, Howard Booth has nowhere to stay except with his sister Mary. Mary's stuffy husband Trevor doesn't trust Howard as far as he can throw him, and with good reason. Howard is basically good at heart, but can't seem to resist putting his scheming ideas into practice. His plans inevitably go wrong at the worst possible moment. *The Bounder*'s intricate stories pile one complication on top of another, making it virtually impossible for Howard to extract himself from crises of his own making. Somehow his quick thinking and endless supply of white lies manage to pull him through. He is a master of talking his way out of some very tight spots indeed.

In a wonderfully complex episode, "Howard at the Majestic," Howard has totally forgotten Mary and Trevor's tenth wedding anniversary. Of course, rather than appear thoughtless, he announces that he has made dinner reservations for all of them at the expensive Majestic Restaurant. From that point on, he has to somehow provide an elegant dinner for his sister and her husband without the benefit of a table reservation or money. Once at the restaurant, they mistakenly enter a private party room where an old school rugby team is holding a reunion. Howard makes the most of the situation by dispensing drinks to the party guests, and even ordering a few for Trevor and Mary. Soon he is regaling the guests with stories about his own heroic sports career, and even offers his opinions about the current team. After a guest mentions how past party crashers have been debagged (the ritual removing of an offender's trousers), Howard realizes he has to seat Trevor and Mary properly. He promptly tries to bribe the maitre d' to get a terrace table. When that doesn't work, he speaks indignantly to the manager, claiming to be with Mountjoy from "the head office." The manager

Howard snatches a salmon from the hands of a rugby team in a desperate attempt to maintain his latest scheme. *Yorkshire Television*

quickly seats them at a nice table in the dining room. As the anniversary couple dance, Howard is discovered to be a fraud and their table is unceremoniously cleared. His explanation to Trevor and Mary is that he found a caterpillar in his dish, and ordered it all taken away. He suggests they try another restaurant, but Mary refuses to leave. Howard then encourages them to dance again, hastily sets up a table outside on the terrace, and sneaks back to the rugby reunion to steal some food. When he doesn't return with enough to make a meal, he ventures into the main dining room posing as a waiter. He even removes a plate right out from under a customer, claiming the dish is no good, and apologizes for the inconvenience. Trevor catches him, causing Howard to "confess" his moonlighting as a waiter. He then sneaks back into the reunion party to smuggle out a plate of salmon. Called to make a speech to the group, he does a convincing job, just in time to elude the manager again. He brings the salmon dish outside to the chilly Trevor and Mary. When he hears the rugby club members looking for their food thief, Howard quickly asks Mary for a dance, leaving Trevor alone with the salmon plate. As they dance, they hear a commotion from the terrace and watch Trevor's trousers fly into the room.

In "On Approval," Howard continues his relentless pursuit of Laura, the attractive and wealthy widow next door. He has been surprisingly inept at securing her affections, thanks to his compulsive fibbing. "Just try to be yourself," suggests Mary. "If you can remember what that is."

Once he has Laura alone, Howard can't help but spin a tale about his hefty Swiss bank account. Laura once more sees through the deceit. In an effort to win her over, Howard returns home the next day to show Trevor a bracelet studded with diamonds and rubies. He then explains that it's worth 7,000 pounds, but he got it on approval by using Trevor as a reference! Trevor wants Howard to take it back, but Howard is convinced that Laura will reject it anyway. "Laura's that kind of woman—you can't buy her love." Much to his horror, though, she accepts the bracelet gladly.

At first, Howard tries to convince Laura that she shouldn't keep the bracelet, although he keeps putting his own words into innocent bystander Trevor's mouth ("Are you trying to say it's a shade vulgar, Trevor?") His story that the bracelet is cursed also fails to move Laura. In desperation, he persuades Trevor to help him "steal" the bracelet while Laura is out. Trevor skulks into the bedroom and searches the dresser for it, unaware that Laura is reclining on her bed behind him, reading a book. She silently watches him for a moment before he catches sight of her in the mirror. Howard then comes in, sees that they've been caught, and offers her yet another feeble story. Trevor then suggests that Howard start an argument with Laura to get her angry enough to throw the bracelet back at him. It finally works, but Laura is so angry that Howard isn't sure she will ever speak to him again.

The plots for *The Bounder* tend to be more intricate than Eric Chappell's other sitcoms, and indeed more intricate than most sitcoms in general. "I think yes, they had to be," he said. "It was very difficult. It had to be a confidence trick, it had to work within a domestic environment. It couldn't be a big scam, it had to be a modest deception, and he couldn't really do anything terrible, or he couldn't be lovable. Whatever he did had to be fairly harmless and yet amusing and interesting."

Peter Bowles and George Cole won joint Best Actor awards at the 1982 Pye Colour Television Awards for their work on *The Bounder*. In addition, Chappell won an award for creator of the best male comedy role. The series also achieved impressive ratings, with six of the first seven episodes landing in the Top Ten. So why were only fourteen episodes produced? An unusual turn of events holds the answer.

Shortly before beginning work on *The Bounder*, George Cole had starred in a comedy for

Laura (Isla Blair) loves her new bracelet even more than Howard bargained for.
Yorkshire Television

Thames TV called *Minder*, which hadn't been very successful. While Cole was working on *The Bounder*, Thames decided to repeat the first series of *Minder*, which suddenly caught on with the public. As Peter Bowles recalled, "This repeat was so successful that they decided they would do some more *Minder*s, which they weren't sure they were going to do at all. So there was George playing second fiddle to me, and was suddenly being offered a whole new ballgame of *Minder*, an hour-long show, so he decided to go along with that. And suddenly the duo thing had gone, so they decided they couldn't continue [*The Bounder*]. *Minder* was a very, very big hit here. It ran for fifteen years." It's unfortunate *The Bounder* enjoyed such a short life in comparison.

THE YOUNG ONES

BBC
1982-1984
12 Episodes

Written by Ben Elton, Rik Mayall, Lise
*   Mayer*
Produced by Paul Jackson

Available on home video in the U.S.

Cast:

RIK . . . . Rik Mayall
VYVYAN . . . . Adrian Edmondson
NEIL . . . . Nigel Planer
MIKE . . . . Christopher Ryan
BALOWSKY FAMILY . . . . Alexei Sayle

Rik (Rik Mayall) launches into a typical vein-popping rant as Vyvyan (Ade Edmondson), Neil (Nigel Planer), and Mike (Christopher Ryan) look on without much sympathy.
BBC Worldwide

The Young Ones is as much a live-action cartoon as it is a sitcom. It has proven to be perhaps the most influential of the alternative comedy series of the 1980s despite its total output of only twelve episodes. Its rebellious attitude toward all things "establishment" made it a particular favorite among teens and twentysomethings on both sides of the Atlantic.

The main cast members first made a splash on television on the comedy/variety show *Boom Boom, Out Go the Lights*, produced by Paul Jackson. This break led to *The Young Ones*, which Jackson also produced and directed (he and production manager Ed Bye would work together again several years later on *Red Dwarf*).

The action in *The Young Ones* takes place in a run-down house worthy of condemnation by the Board of Health. Its inhabitants, all ostensibly college students, are Rik, a loud, obnoxious Marxist revolutionary; Vyvyan, an even louder and more obnoxious heavy metal punk with spiky orange hair; Neil, a tall, slouching sad sack with what could kindly be called a low self-esteem problem; and Mike, a laid-back, halfway sensible guy who

remains unfazed by any and all incidents, including the occasional explosion, within the house.

The barely-contained anarchy that permeates each episode includes surreal sight gags (talking appliances, socks, assorted vermin commenting on the action) and disgusting sight gags (garbage served for dinner, decapitations), and plenty of stylized violence (Vyvyan hitting Rik and/or Neil on the head to relieve his boredom). Toilet humor and foul language infest the dialogue. The gags come at a fast and furious pace, with barely a wisp of a plot in each episode to string it all together. Parodies of other TV shows are also thrown into the mix, as are guest rock groups appearing from out of nowhere to perform their best-known hits. And yet, almost miraculously, this show manages to be genuinely funny, if only due to the over-the-top nature of the show. Ed Bye recalled, "When I first read the scripts, I knew this was dynamite, I knew this was dead funny. Very radical. It was one of those things where people either got it or they didn't."

The best and brightest of Britain's "alternative" comedy performers made guest appearances on the show, including Mel Smith and Griff Rhys-Jones,

Fry and Laurie, French and Saunders, Robbie Coltrane, Emma Thompson, and series creator Ben Elton.

The episode "Bambi" has the boys venturing to the laundromat for the first time. Not only does their stinking laundry drive the other customers out on the street for air, but the washing machine spits out their clothes in protest. Vyvyan decides that "This calls for a careful blend of psychology and extreme violence." He casually approaches the washer with a handful of clothes and the tempting line, "Oh, la de da, look what I have here. All of Felicity Kendal's underwear, and it needs a good wash." The machine eagerly opens its door with a perverted giggle as the others stuff their offensive clothes inside and force it closed. Their only problem is that none of them has brought any coins needed to turn it on. Back at home, they vow never to do their laundry again. "What do you mean, *again*?" asks Mike.

Later, they take a train to appear on the TV quiz show *University Challenge*, for which they were chosen to represent Scumbag College. Rik and Neil try to cram for it by studying useless trivia books. Vyvyan, curious as to why passengers are warned not to stick their heads out the windows of the moving train, does just that, only to lose his head as the train enters a tunnel. His headless body pulls the emergency cord, and once outside, accidentally kicks Vyvyan's talking head down the tracks, much to his annoyance (this gruesome gag, obviously played for laughs, looks surprisingly realistic!).

The boys make their way to a television studio and meet Bambi (Griff Rhys-Jones, in a parody of real-life *University Challenge* host Bamber Gascoigne), and naturally wreak havoc during the show's taping. Their competitors are the rich snobs of Footlights College, Oxbridge (played by Emma Thompson, Stephen Fry, Hugh Laurie, and Ben Elton). The proceedings end with the inevitable splash of violence courtesy of Vyvyan. After stomping on the head of his competitor seated below, he sets off a smoke bomb to top off the day.

Nigel Planer, in an interview with *The Guardian*, maintains that "*The Young Ones*, despite being revolutionary, was a two-act comedy within a half an hour, with a premise and a conclusion. My theory is that all sitcoms are like this." The series'

imitators have attempted to become anti-sitcoms, but Planer feels they've missed the point. "[Ben Elton] is actually a very traditional writer in his scripts and novels. In spite of appearing to deconstruct the sitcom, he actually reinvented the form."

Production manager Ed Bye added, "While the jokes and gags were absurd and juvenile in one respect, in another respect it was a lot more realistic than anything else that was going on in television. Everything else in terms of comedy was a pair of French windows, a sofa, and people running around worrying about the shopping. Very middle class. So it was a radical move in that respect, and very Pythonesque in some ways."

The Young Ones made a splash in the U.S. in 1984, when MTV began airing the program to the delight of its key demographic group, i.e., young rock fans with a taste for irreverence.

After *The Young Ones*, Rik Mayall and Adrian Edmondson teamed up to write and star in television projects such as *The Dangerous Brothers* and *Bottom*, as well as making guest appearances on programs such as *The Black Adder* and *Absolutely Fabulous*. Mayall also starred in his own series, *The New Statesman*, written by Laurence Marks and Maurice Gran (*Goodnight Sweetheart*). Alexei Sayle, who appears in *The Young Ones* as the boys' landlord Mr. Balowsky and as various other members of the Balowsky family, took his obscenity-filled stand-up comedy routines and cleaned up his act just enough to star in his own BBC sketch show, *Alexei Sayle's Stuff*.

The Young Ones in a rare tranquil moment.
BBC Worldwide

THE BLACK ADDER

BBC
1983-1989
24 Episodes, 1 Special

The Black Adder (1983, 6 episodes)
Written by Richard Curtis and Rowan Atkinson
Directed by Martin Shardlow
Produced by John Lloyd

Black Adder II (1986, 6 episodes)
Written by Richard Curtis and Ben Elton
Directed by Mandie Fletcher
Produced by John Lloyd

Blackadder the Third (1987, 6 episodes)
Written by Richard Curtis and Ben Elton
Directed by Mandie Fletcher
Produced by John Lloyd

Blackadder Goes Forth (1989, 6 episodes)
Written by Richard Curtis and Ben Elton
Directed by Richard Bowden
Produced by John Lloyd

Available on home video in the U.S.

The original Edmund, fore-father of his opportunistic descendants. It must be in the genes. *BBC Worldwide*

Cast:

Edmund Blackadder	Rowan Atkinson
Baldrick	Tony Robinson
Queen Elizabeth	Miranda Richardson
Melchett	Stephen Fry
George	Hugh Laurie
Nursie (series 1, 2)	Patsy Byrne
Percy (series 1, 2),	
Captain Darling (series 4)	Tim McInnerny

When considering the popularity and success of the *Black Adder* series, we should note from the start how different it is from any American (or British) sitcom—the very fact that it takes place in a succes-sion of historical time periods makes it an especially ambitious and unique series.

Americans are not known to be terribly well versed in history, including our own. Perhaps our collective ignorance is one reason why a historical or period sitcom has never succeeded here. Mel Brooks attempted a Robin Hood satire in 1975 with *When Things Were Rotten*. This series, done in typical Brooks style, received low ratings and was canceled after three months. *Happy Days* was set in the 1950s and was undeniably successful, but the period setting eventually became secondary to the gargantuan popularity of the Fonzie character. Rob Reiner made a heartfelt attempt in 1978 with *Free Country*, a series about newly arrived immigrants in New York at the turn of the century, but it didn't survive. *Best of the West*, a spoof of life in the Old West, lasted a single season in 1981-82. More recently, at the beginning of the 1998-99 season, UPN offered the period sitcom *The Secret Diary of Desmond Pfeiffer*. The title character served as a White House butler during the Lincoln administration. Jokes referring to slavery, sex in the Oval Office, and other topics of questionable taste sealed the program's fate. Critics complained more about the show's inept writing and acting, while African-American groups charged racism. *Pfeiffer* died a quick death.

Compare this record with the success of *The Black Adder* and its subsequent incarnations. Millions of British viewers accepted a comedy series taking place initially in the Middle Ages, then progressing through history with each set of six episodes, up to and including World War I. Of course, the main appeal of the series is that of brilliant comedian Rowan Atkinson as the mean-spirited and terminally sarcastic Edmund Blackadder (political correctness need never be a consideration in developing a British comedy series, thank God). The eccentric supporting characters are equally delightful. As we move ahead in time from one series to the next, the cast regulars play the descendants of the characters from the *previous* series, creating a strong continuity.

Not long after the satirical sketch program *Not the Nine O'Clock News* ended production, the BBC asked co-star Rowan Atkinson and co-writer Richard Curtis to come up with a sitcom. Atkinson wanted to do a sitcom, but he and Curtis soon found the assignment rather intimidating, especially as they considered the sitcom standard previously set by *Fawlty Towers*.

Producer John Lloyd recalls that the germ of the idea for the series began when Atkinson and Curtis decided to attempt some kind of period piece, and went off to France to work on a story premise about a king and his friends. "*Black Adder* was meant to be his stab at a *Fawlty Towers*, as it were," says Lloyd. "I think in a way you can see the relationship between Black Adder and Baldrick is similar to Fawlty and Manuel."

Each series revels in the juxtaposition of literate dialogue and broad slapstick, especially in the second, third, and fourth series. The original *Black Adder* series of six episodes enjoyed a lavish budget, spent mostly on location scenes and ornate period costumes. Unfortunately, these early episodes also tend to be a bit crude and over the top. Scenes are broadly acted and often shouted, especially in the case of Brian Blessed as Richard IV. Our "hero" Edmund is a weasel and a coward, but has a talent for devious plotting to improve his station in life. He dubs himself the Black Adder (as in snake). His manservant Baldrick is mangy and pitifully dim-witted, yet eager to please his master. He rarely does, however.

Unimpressed by the results, the BBC nearly canceled the second series before it began. In order to win a reprieve, producer John Lloyd promised significant changes. First, the budget was slashed, relegating all taping to the studio. This was actually a plus for Atkinson's performance, since he could sharpen his timing by working off the studio audience's responses. In addition, comedian/writer Ben Elton joined the show as co-writer, and helped transform Edmund Blackadder's character from sniveling to snide.

"The freshness that Ben brought to Richard's exhaustion meant that they absolutely wrote half the series each," said John Lloyd. "The chemistry produced absolutely brilliant work, and they became very close very quickly, and they developed this completely unique and original writing and characterization style."

Elton was fond of the first series but felt that Atkinson's character was too unappealing and that the show should be written to attract a young, vibrant audience. He and Curtis suggested the setting be updated to the Elizabethan period. With *Black Adder II*, the series hit its stride.

The time is the sixteenth century. Lord Edmund Blackadder is a not-so-humble servant to the spoiled, screechy Queen Elizabeth. Unlike his original ancestor, *this* Blackadder is an erudite, sarcastic descendant. He treats friends and foes alike with casual contempt, and even insults the Queen to her face without her realizing he's doing it. Baldrick remains, as always, oddly loyal to the man who considers him little more than a missing rung on the evolutionary ladder. Lord Percy also submits to routine humiliation on behalf of Lord Edmund.

The difference in response to the original series and *Black Adder II* was like night and day. The series was now on a roll. John Lloyd felt that since the show had moved through time once already, the trend should continue. The writers were content to keep things as they were. "I said that doesn't seem balanced to me, I think we should move on," Lloyd recalled. "And also it gives it legs, because you're never gonna get bored with a series that moves through history all the time. It's almost like reincarnation. You can have essentially the same characters, but the freshness of giving Blackadder a different job on each occasion that it brings to the writing is longer lasting than, say, *Fawlty Towers.*"

Blackadder the Third places a further descendant of Edmund Blackadder in the Regency period, circa 1760–1815. The Blackadder family fortunes are not what they once were, and Edmund Blackadder has swallowed his pride to serve as butler to the cheerful but hopelessly idiotic Prince George. The job is made especially difficult by the fact that George is, in his own words, "thick as a whale omelette." Edmund has to keep on his toes to meet the challenge of avoiding one disaster after another, often brought on by George's and/or Baldrick's bottomless stupidity.

In "Ink and Incompatibility," Dr. Samuel Jonson (Robbie Coltrane) visits Prince George to ask for his patronage of Jonson's new dictionary. George is a bit miffed by the absence of a juicy plot. Edmund congratulates Jonson on his achievement, and slyly tosses in a few words that Jonson has either overlooked or never heard of. Jonson has expressed interest in a novel written by one Gertrude Perkins, who, unknown to all others, is Edmund himself. Edmund encourages George to patronize the dictionary that Jonson has left behind, only to learn that Baldrick has fed it to the fire in the fireplace. The oblivious George is content to announce, "Now that I've got my fire, I'm as happy as a Frenchman who's invented a pair of

Black Adder II: (*clockwise from top*) **Lord Melchett (Stephen Fry), Percy (Tim McInnerny), Edmund Blackadder (Rowan Atkinson), Baldrick (Tony Robinson), Nursie (Patsy Byrne), and Queen Elizabeth (Miranda Richardson).** *BBC Worldwide*

self-removing trousers." A concerned Edmund hurries to Jonson's hangout, Mrs. Miggins's pie shop, to steal a second copy of the dictionary. There he runs into Jonson who asks for the dictionary he left with George. There is no second copy, he informs Edmund.

Edmund returns to George to announce, "I will be leaving immediately for Nepal, where I intend to live as a goat." Baldrick's cunning plan is to rewrite the dictionary overnight. Edmund labors all night without success, and must confess the next day to Jonson that the dictionary was burnt. Just then George enters with it, proclaims its excellence

Blackadder the Third. Edmund and Baldrick attend to royal ignoramus George (Hugh Laurie). *BBC Worldwide*

later co-starred in the well-received series *Jeeves and Wooster*). Writer Richard Curtis helped create *Comic Relief*, Ben Elton tried his hand at stand-up comedy and became very successful, and Lloyd himself started producing the extremely popular comedy satire show *Splitting Image*. "So, instead of a bunch of friends coming together to do a little sit-com," he said, "you suddenly had a lot of seriously famous people, among the most successful people in British comedy coming back into the same room and having to give up a huge amount of territory." The clash of egos created a few tense moments, but maintaining the overall quality of the series remained the paramount goal of all involved. Creative differences managed to get ironed out, and the team camaraderie won out in the end. "And usually by the fifth or sixth episode everyone was wishing we were running twenty-two episodes instead of a measly six!" said Lloyd.

In the two-year gap between series three and four, the team presented a holiday special, *Blackadder's Christmas Carol.* Here we find a sur-prisingly chipper Ebenezer Blackadder preparing to celebrate a modest Christmas with his assistant Baldrick, until a succession of visits from greedy friends and relatives leaves him without his dinner or holiday treats. Later that night, a Christmas spirit (Robbie Coltrane) visits Blackadder, compli-ments him on his unerring civility, and shows him visions of his mean-spirited ancestors. Their con-niving ways actually impress Blackadder, and by the next morning, he is a new man, albeit cold and ruthless, in the finest tradition of his forefathers.

Blackadder Goes Forth takes us to the battle-fields of France during World War I. Naturally, Captain Edmund Blackadder is forever scheming to find a way out of the trenches and into a cushier, safer post for the duration. Like his ancestors, he doesn't make many friends along the way.

In "Corporal Punishment," Edmund must deal with difficulties in the army's communications system. The phone in his bunker keeps ringing with wrong numbers as he and George await a new set of orders to advance on the enemy. When a car-rier pigeon arrives outside, Edmund shoots it, but the message attached to the bird's leg declares that due to the communication problems, shooting car-rier pigeons is now a court martial offense. Edmund quickly eats the evidence. Soon afterward, the boisterous General Melchett and sniveling

and agrees to patronize it. Seizing the moment, Edmund confesses that he is indeed the novelist Gertrude Perkins, but Baldrick tells him that *that* book has been burnt. They all wander out of the room as Baldrick stays behind and unwittingly (how else?) tosses Jonson's dictionary into the fire.

Blackadder the Third won a BAFTA award for Best Light Entertainment series in 1988. The contin-uing *Black Adder* exploits grew in popularity with each new series, achieving its highest rating (11.7 mil-lion viewers) with *Blackadder Goes Forth* in 1989. The Audience Appreciation numbers also grew, again reaching a peak with that final series (which, like its predecessor, won a BAFTA award). Developments among the cast members off-screen throughout the mid-1980s almost put the series itself in jeopardy.

"People started to get seriously famous wearing their own hats," recalled John Lloyd. Atkinson's fame and popularity continued to grow. Fry and Laurie began their own sketch series (and

Captain Darling arrive to discover that Edmund committed his transgression against the General's boyhood pet pigeon, Speckled Jim. The apoplectic Melchett has Edmund arrested pending a court martial and firing squad.

Edmund sends for a famous lawyer to defend him, but thanks to Baldrick's latest botch-up, George has taken the case despite freely admitting his legal incompetence. Edmund tells him, "I need to make a case as airtight as a mermaid's brassiere." However, his hopes for a fair trial are dashed when Melchett as chief judge repeatedly refers to Edmund as the "Flanders Pigeon Murderer." George, despite his inept courtroom skills, has a great time as Edmund's lawyer. When the prosecutor, Captain Darling, calls General Melchett as a witness, Edmund's fate is soon sealed. Fortunately for him though, a last-minute reprieve from the Minister of War (who happens to be George's Uncle Rupert) saves Edmund from a friendly but determined firing squad.

The final episode of *Blackadder Goes Forth* proves to be surprisingly poignant, even dramatic. We witness Captain Blackadder, George, Baldrick, and Darling on the losing end of the battle at the front line. They express their fears but, with a typical British stiff upper lip, resign themselves to their impending fate and make their final move over the hill to face certain death. Even this irreverent comedy proved adept at making its own statement about the horrors of war.

Several ideas for a fifth *Black Adder* series were discussed and rejected. Richard Curtis came up with *The Blackadder Five*, about a 1960s rock group somewhat akin to the Dave Clark Five, and featuring a drummer named Bald Rick. Other ideas, such as going back in time to *The Six Wives of Blackadder*, never got past the talking stage. (Curtis later wrote the screenplay for the feature film hit *Four Weddings and a Funeral*.)

Blackadder Goes Forth. Duty calls: (*left to right*) George, Captain Darling, General Melchett, Edmund, and Baldrick. *BBC Worldwide*

Not long after *The Black Adder* was put to rest, Rowan Atkinson found further success with his wildly popular *Mr. Bean* series. Co-written by Atkinson, Curtis, and Robin Driscoll, most episodes contain two or three segments, each totally visual and crammed with inventive sight gags, with a minimum of dialogue. Mr. Bean is a childlike, highly imaginative loner who seems perfectly content with his own company. He possesses a skewed logic and regularly finds ingenious ways of devising on-the-spot solutions to his self-made predicaments. As Mr. Bean, Atkinson's performance is actually very reminiscent of comedy legend Stan Laurel, although Bean tends to be more selfish and at times a tad annoying. In 1997 Atkinson starred in the feature film, *Bean: The Movie*, based on the series. The film was directed by Mel Smith, Atkinson's fellow *Not the Nine O'Clock News* alumnus.

Don't Wait Up

BBC
1983-1990
39 Episodes

Written by George Layton
Produced and directed by Harold Snoad

Cast:

TOM LATIMER	Nigel Havers
TOBY LATIMER	Tony Britten
HELEN	Jane How
ANGELA	Dinah Sheridan
MADELINE	Susan Skipper
CHARLES	Richard Heffer (later Simon Williams)

Tom (Nigel Havers), Angela (Dinah Sheridan), and Toby (Tony Britten). *BBC Worldwide*

Don't Wait Up was the first series George Layton created and wrote on his own, after becoming well-known to British audiences as an actor and part-time writer for the popular series *Doctor in the House*. He also contributed scripts for *Robin's Nest* and appeared in David Croft's series *It Ain't Half Hot, Mum*.

The premise of *Don't Wait Up* has been described as a sort of British version of *The Odd Couple*, but that would be oversimplifying it. Here, the odd couple consists of Tom Latimer, a young, recently divorced doctor, and his father Toby, also a doctor. As the series opens, Tom is shocked to learn that his parents have not only separated, but that his father intends to move in with him for the time being. Tom can't refuse of course, but he's determined to get his parents Toby and Angela back together, for his sake as well as theirs. Until that happens, though, the two Doctor Latimers must share the same flat and try not to cramp each other's style. As an attractive young man in search of a new mate, Tom soon learns just how cramped his style (not to mention his apartment) can get.

In one episode, Tom attempts a romantic evening with his girlfriend Madeline, who is also Toby's receptionist. Toby attends a doctor's stag dinner that evening, leaving Tom with a few hours to work his charms. Although Madeline is at first receptive to his efforts, she becomes worried that Toby might arrive home early and interrupt them. Tom gets increasingly frustrated. "Here I am, thirty-one years old," he says, "I'm behaving like a nervous teenager trying to get a quick grope before my dad comes home." After returning later from taking Madeline home, Tom realizes that Toby is still out. The next morning, he brings coffee to his father's room but to his horror, Toby hasn't returned yet. He finally comes through the front door. Tom berates him (in an amusing father-son role reversal), and although he won't admit it, is convinced that Toby has spent the night with a woman. "I'm not the least bit interested in your sordid love life," Tom tells him, "But I just think that you might have the good manners to tell me when you're not coming home, so that I could organize my *own* sordid love life!" His real concern, however, is how Toby's affair would affect the chances of reconciliation with Angela.

The next day, an angry Madeline, who has heard the real story from Toby, calls Tom to inform him that his father was in fact busy saving a man's life at the dinner the previous evening. She adds that she doesn't want to see Tom again. A contrite Tom apologizes to Toby for jumping to conclusions. They patch things up and go out to dinner, then decide to stop by Angela's for a late-night visit. Just as they arrive, they spot a young man letting himself into the house with his own key. Father and son are now both suspicious that *Angela* is having the affair. Toby is reminded the next day that the mysterious man is an Australian exchange student, Jonathan Spencer, who had long ago arranged to stay with the Latimers. Tom finds out only after berating Jonathan on the phone. He goes over later in the day to apologize, and asks Jonathan if he thinks he'll enjoy living in London. "It's hard to tell," he replies, "After all, I only arrived here an hour ago."

George Layton's talent for intricate plotting is further on display in an episode full of mishaps for Toby. Tom's associate Charles encourages Tom to go out and meet women, even if it feels a bit uncomfortable. Much to his surprise, Tom manages to chat up a beautiful young blonde named Inga in a wine bar. They go to a disco and then to his flat. Toby is impressed, but warns his son that Inga is Charles' very young au pair. Later that night, Tom's nightmare about his ex-wife Helen leads to a chat with Toby. "Can you imagine Mom with somebody else?" Tom says offhandedly. Disturbed by the idea, Toby throws on some old clothes and takes a late night walk, ending up at his house. He lets himself in, setting off the alarm that he can't shut off. Angela is away, and Toby has no identification on him to satisfy the police. He has no choice but to spend the night in jail. Tom has to bail out his disheveled father the next morning.

That night, Tom agrees to babysit for Charles and briefly meets the new au pair—a big, brawny girl named Berta—who will take over for him later in the evening. When an ill neighbor needs his help, Tom calls Toby to take over and watch the children. Berta then arrives, and mistakes Toby for an intruder. She

slugs him unconscious, and he's arrested again. Tom must bail him out a second time. The look on his father's whiskered, dejected face when he's brought out says it all. He needs a vacation and decides to take one. While packing, he gives Tom the car keys to go fill up the car at the gas station. Leaving the house with a black bag, Toby is confronted by two policemen in need of directions. His nervous babbling makes the cops more suspicious with each utterance. Tom must return to the police station yet again to pick up his father. The incident has made Toby late for his plane, so he speeds down the highway, only to hear a distant police siren approaching from behind. "Don't worry," he tells Tom with a manic gleam in his eye, "I'll lose them."

Don't Wait Up won the TRIC (Television Radio Industries Club) Best Comedy award in 1990.

Producer Harold Snoad has always enjoyed George Layton's writing style:

> I'm a great admirer because he writes not only funny shows, but he always has good episode stories. There's a plot and a subplot, and at the end of the episode all the [loose ends] have been tied together . . . George and I got on very well together, and *Don't Wait Up* was a great success over here.

Layton's work may enjoy much admiration, but the creative process isn't always easy. "Oh, it's a terrible strain," he said. "I mean, I wrote six series of *Don't Wait Up*, and it nearly killed me! . . . So much effort goes into writing that I really do feel happy when people say 'Oh, I loved your show' or 'Aren't you the writer of that,' because writers are very anonymous. I think they get very little recognition, actually."

No Place Like Home

BBC
1983-1987
43 Episodes

Written by Jon Watkins
Produced by Robin Nash

Cast:

Arthur Crabtree	William Gaunt
Beryl Crabtree	Patricia Garwood
Lorraine	Beverly Adams
Raymond	Daniel Hill
Paul	Steven Watson
Tracy	Dee Sadler
Vera Botting	Marcia Warren
Trevor Botting	Michael Sharvell-Martin
Nigel	Martin Clunes

Arthur (William Gaunt) and Beryl (Patricia Garwood) share a moment in Arthur's greenhouse getaway. *BBC Worldwide*

The first episode of this domestic sitcom presents Arthur and Beryl Crabtree, a pleasant couple in their mid-forties, who have finally seen the last of their four offspring leave the nest. Their son Nigel is on his way to veterinary school in Edinburgh. At last, for the first time in over twenty years, mother and father have their home truly to themselves. Arthur relishes the thought but Beryl is already suffering from empty-nest syndrome. Arthur is determined to celebrate, so he prepares an old-fashioned romantic evening featuring a candlelight dinner (providing he can cook) and whatever else captures their imagination.

Before they can get comfortable, the doorbell rings. Nigel has returned, deciding vet school isn't for him after all. Their daughter Lorraine calls to say she's had a fight with her fiancé Raymond and wants to come home. In quick order, the other siblings Paul and Tracy return for a variety of reasons, and before Arthur and Beryl know it, their house is again buzzing with activity.

In a later episode we meet Raymond, Lorraine's new moronic husband (played by Daniel Hill, also known as Harvey Banes on *Waiting for God*). Arthur can't stand the sniveling Raymond, who insists on calling him "Dad," but he also knows Lorraine wants to work on the shaky marriage, and therefore tries to tolerate Raymond's irritating ways.

Whenever things get too hectic, Arthur retreats to the quiet of his greenhouse in the backyard, where he's often joined by his next-door neighbor Trevor. Trevor and his wife Vera have no children but instead keep a veritable zoo of wayward animals under their roof. Vera is also an especially talkative and nosy neighbor who spends more time having coffee in the Crabtree's kitchen than in her own.

In the late 1990s, American viewers saw William Gaunt reappear on their screens in the sitcom *Next of Kin*, co-starring Penelope Keith.

Martin Clunes (Nigel) has appeared in several sitcoms throughout the 1980s and 1990s, and co-starred in the extremely popular hit sitcom *Men Behaving Badly* (which was later adapted in the United States and ran for two seasons).

'Allo, 'Allo!

BBC-1
1984 –1992
83 Episodes, 2 Specials

Written by Jeremy Lloyd and David Croft
(series 1–6)
Jeremy Lloyd and Paul Adam
(series 7–9)
Produced by David Croft

Cast:

Rene Artois	Gorden Kaye
Edith Artois	Carmen Silvera
Yvette	Vicki Michelle
Alphonse	Kenneth Connor
Michelle	Kirsten Cooke
LeClerc	Jack Haig
Colonel von Strohm	Richard Marner
Hans Geering	Sam Kelly
General von Klinkerhoffen	Hilary Minster
Lieutenant Gruber	Guy Siner
Crabtree	Arthur Bostrom
Herr Flick	Richard Gibson
von Smallhausen	John Louis Mansi
Helga	Kim Hartman
Fanny	Rose Hill
Mimi	Sue Hodge
Alberto Bertorelli	Gavin Richards
Fairfax	John D. Collins
Carstairs	Nicholas Frankau
Denise LaRoc	Moira Foot

(*Left to right*): Resistance leader Michelle (Kirsten Cooke) with Monsieur Alphonse (Kenneth Connor), Edith (Carmen Silvera), and Rene (Gorden Kaye). Michelle begins each of her updates with her trademark warning, "Listen very carefully, I shall say this only once . . ."
BBC Worldwide

Writer/producer David Croft had already enjoyed years of tremendous success with sitcoms such as *Dad's Army, Are You Being Served?*, and several others by the time he and partner Jeremy Lloyd created their farcical masterpiece *'Allo, 'Allo!*. For nine series, this shamelessly silly comic soap opera set in German-occupied France never passed up an opportunity to go for a big laugh, regardless of—anything. Each and every episode is crammed with

sight gags, plot twists, and ludicrous dialogue. The colorful characters and absurd situations create an unstoppable momentum from one episode to the next. *'Allo, 'Allo!* is a marvel of comic invention, praised by both critics and fans around the world.

The sprawling story revolves around the most unlikely of heroes, Rene Artois (pronounced "Atwah"), a café owner in the small French town of Nouvion. Rene's efforts to maintain a reasonably normal life under German occupation go awry in the first episode. The French Resistance, led by a beautiful young woman named Michelle, has designated his café as a safehouse for escapees. Rene's protests go unheeded, and before he knows it, he is performing a delicate balancing act between pacifying the local German officers and assisting the Resistance in their efforts to sabotage the Third Reich in France. Rene is the first to admit he's a coward and isn't shy about expressing his reluctance to get involved with Michelle's harebrained schemes. Like it or not though, he always finds himself in the middle of them.

'Allo, 'Allo! is in part a satire of the BBC drama series *Secret Army* which aired from 1977 to 1979. That program dramatized the dangerous efforts of the French Resistance during the war, and featured a café owner named Albert. Its premise plus a few of the original characters were reinvented as *'Allo, 'Allo!*, but the similarities end there.

Throughout the large cast of characters (some of which do not appear in the earlier episodes), each has a wonderfully individual personality:

Edith Artois—Rene's wife, helpmate, and self-appointed cabaret singer, whose singing voice prompts the customers to stuff wedges of cheese in their ears.

Yvette and Maria (later replaced by Mimi)—Rene's youthful waitresses who harbor a burning desire for their boss. He gladly satisfies their needs.

Monsieur Alphonse—Local undertaker, Resistance fighter, Edith's suitor, and Rene's friend and/or rival, depending on the day of the week.

LeClerc—Elderly piano player, forger, burglar, master of disguise. Unfortunately, he performs all of these tasks miserably.

Fairfax and Carstairs—Clueless British airmen forever hiding and/or disguised while awaiting their return to England.

Officer Crabtree—British Resistance fighter disguised as a local police gendarme. His clumsy attempts to speak French often result in embarrassing mispronunciations.

Colonel von Strohm and Captain Hans Geering—Buffoonish local German officers and uneasy allies of Rene. They command marginal respect only when threatening to shoot someone.

Lieutenant Gruber—Soft-hearted German lieutenant who has an obvious crush on Rene.

Herr Flick and von Smallhausen—Herr Flick is a proud, menacing Gestapo officer and von Smallhausen is his creepy, submissive assistant. Both sport black leather trench coats and pronounced limps.

Helga—Herr Flick's blonde girlfriend (their macabre "romance" often involves leather undergarments and bondage-like games) who doubles as Colonel von Strohm's secretary.

Captain Alberto Bertorelli—Dim-witted but extremely confident Italian officer and self-professed ladies' man.

Denise LaRoc—Leader of the Communist Resistance in France and Rene's long-lost love.

The busy first episode of *'Allo, 'Allo!*, like that of any other series, begins by establishing its setting and introducing us to most of the main characters, but it does so with several ingenious twists. We witness many of the characters meeting each other for the first time, usually amid a great deal of confusion. The highlight comes with Rene and Yvette's initial encounter with the British airmen in the back room of the café. Even though the audience hears everything in English, Fairfax and Carstairs can't understand a word Rene says, since he is speaking French. Likewise, Rene and Yvette can't understand the airmen. They all resort to gestures and pantomime in a hilarious attempt to communicate with each other, but only succeed in piling one misunderstanding on top of another. Michelle finally comes to the rescue by addressing the airmen in English (usually beginning with "Okay, chaps . . ."). A short time later, LeClerc arrives (having been blown out of a prison cell by the Resistance) with a set of code words so Rene can easily identify him. Their exchange of encoded phrases ("Do you have a light?" "I have no matches," etc.) is foiled by the unsuspecting Lieutenant Gruber, who interrupts to offer a light and extra matches to the frustrated duo.

The plotline of *'Allo, 'Allo!* might be likened to the Big Bang Theory: The plot elements established in the first episode expand outward from that point at a dizzying rate. It is impossible to capture all of the interwoven storylines, but here's the starting point.

Colonel von Strohm and Captain Geering have stolen several valuable items including a priceless painting, *The Fallen Madonna with the Big Boobies*, to sell after the war. Herr Flick of the

The ensemble. Seated (*left to right*): von Smallhausen (John Louis Mansi), Herr Flick (Richard Gibson), General von Klinkerhoffen (Hilary Minster), Colonel von Strohm (Richard Marner), Alphonse (Kenneth Connor), LeClerc (Jack Haig), and Edith's mother Fanny (Rose Hill). Standing are Lieutenant Gruber (Guy Siner), Helga (Kim Hartman), Crabtree (Arthur Bostrom), Alberto Bertorelli (Gavin Richards), Edith (Carmen Silvera), Rene (Gorden Kaye), Mimi (Sue Hodge), Yvette (Vicki Michelle), Carstairs (Nicholas Frankau), Michelle (Kirsten Cooke), and Fairfax (John D. Collins). *BBC Worldwide*

Gestapo has learned of the theft and is determined to find the culprit. His visit to von Strohm and Geering has made them nervous enough to bring the valuables to Rene, ordering him to hide them in his cellar. They tell him that if he refuses, they will expose his café as a safehouse. The painting has now found a new home. Before long, forgeries of it are made and dispersed and eventually hidden inside several hollowed-out sausages (yes, you read that right). In the meantime, the Resistance has installed a shortwave radio in the bedroom of Edith's cranky, bedridden mother. Rene's radio communications are supposed to facilitate the secret return of the airmen back to England but each plan is doomed to fail dismally.

At the opening of each subsequent episode, Rene addresses us directly to review all that has transpired the week before. This, of course, proves very useful in a series with a continuing storyline, but also gives Rene the opportunity to show us how he is the only character who sees the ridiculous nature of the missions he must carry out each week. David Croft says even he sometimes had trouble keeping track of the storyline. "I used to have to ring up my secretary at the start of each series and say 'Where the hell is everyone [in the story]?' It was enormous fun to write."

In ensuing episodes throughout the series' long run, the myriad of situations put the characters in increasingly absurd predicaments, and caused Rene to assume a variety of unconvincing disguises, including those of Heinrich Himmler, a Franciscan friar, and a buxom grande dame concert pianist. And for much of the storyline, Rene must pose as his own twin brother (conveniently also named Rene), after being "executed" by a German firing squad. At one point or another, each and every character makes an appearance in disguise, especially LeClerc, who is so convinced of his own skills that he feels he must take Rene aside and whisper, "Psst! It is I, LeClerc!" Such is the nature of farce.

'Allo, 'Allo! made extensive use of location scenes, giving the series a sprawling, almost epic quality. "Every show we used to go out filming," said David Croft, "and even your top [American] ones never go out of the studio." The outdoor scenes were all shot on film ahead of time, usually in Norfolk, England, and were played to the audience as the studio taping proceeded. The cast members on location needed to time their lines just right so the audience laughter wouldn't drown out the dialogue later. "You get used to it, but it takes a little while," said Gorden Kaye. "I mastered it by the time we got to the end of the run ten years later!"

Susan Belbin was the original production manager for 'Allo, 'Allo! before David Croft handed over the directing reigns to her after the first few series. She has since directed and produced several sitcoms, including the highly-praised *One Foot in the Grave*. Like Gorden Kaye, she is dedicated to the art of comedy for comedy's sake. "It's the hardest thing to do, and when you get it right, the rewards—to hear an audience laugh or applaud, and you know you've done it right, it's so rewarding," she said.

Guy Siner (Lieutenant Gruber) was the only American actor in the 'Allo, 'Allo! cast.

Kenneth Connor (Monsieur Alphonse) starred in several of the wildly popular *Carry On . . .* feature film comedies of the 1950s and 1960s.

Despite its relatively low profile in the U.S., *'Allo, 'Allo!* has been the biggest selling Britcom internationally. It has been sold to more countries than *Fawlty Towers*, and towards the end of its run in 1992 was even purchased to air in Germany. "It hasn't grown in America like *Are You Being Served?* has," David Croft said. "But I think it will grow undoubtedly. The word of mouth will go between stations."

The series has also enjoyed a successful life beyond its incarnation on television. In 1986, a stage version starring most of the television cast members opened at the London Palladium. Record audiences kept it running for six months, twice as long as originally planned. Gorden Kaye was very proud of the stage run. "It would have been easy to take the top three characters and then everybody else's lookalike," he said. "When we were at our height over the six years, playing four years running over Christmas in London, we had ten of the television actors live and in person. We were showing that we could do it for an hour at a time, then [intermission], then another hour . . . the hardest thing about the stage show is that there are no re-takes on stage." The stage show returned the following year and then went on tour in Australia and New Zealand, but the tireless cast first had to tape twenty-six consecutive episodes before embarking on the tour—an unprecedented feat in Britcom history.

Gorden Kaye as Rene. *BBC Worldwide*

Although *'Allo, 'Allo!* would not be the series it is without star Gorden Kaye (who greatly admires the techniques and timing of comedians such as Jack Benny), he himself deflects much of the credit to the writers. "Maybe one day Jeremy Lloyd and David Croft will be thought of as being top class comedy writers," he said. "They're already thought of as that by me, and by the people who work with them now."

THREE UP, TWO DOWN

BBC
1985-1989
25 Episodes

Written by Richard Ommanney
Directed by Mandie Fletcher, John B. Hobbs
Produced by David Askey, John B. Hobbs

Cast:

DAPHNE .... Angela Thorne
SAM .... Michael Elphick
ANGIE .... Lysette Anthony
NICK .... Ray Burdis
GILES BRADSHAW .... Neil Stacy

(*Left to right*): Angie (Lysette Anthony), Nick (Ray Burdis), Sam (Michael Elphick), Daphne (Angela Thorne), and the baby who brought them all together under one roof.
BBC Worldwide

Comedy is conflict. In the right hands, the more clashes that arise between the characters in question, the greater the comedy potential. The core of *Three Up, Two Down* consists of the clash not only between upper class and working class attitudes, but also of two headstrong in-laws.

As the series opens, Nick and Angie have just welcomed their baby into the world. Nick is a struggling commercial photographer, and Angie intends to return to her job in a few weeks' time. They're still desperate for money and hope to renovate and sublet their building's basement flat. The extra income would help pay babysitting fees.

Nick's father Sam is a Cockney working man. He's a widower and soon to be homeless thanks to the wrecking ball scheduled for his present flat. He is a tad rough around the edges but has a true heart of gold. Angie's mother Daphne is the snobbiest of snobs, accustomed to enjoying afternoon teas with her aristocratic lady friends. Both she and Sam have come to town to see their new grandson.

Sam's persistent pleas to have Nick rent him the basement flat in exchange for babysitting duties finally cause Nick to give in. Unknown to the men however, Angie and Daphne have a talk along similar lines in the hospital maternity ward. Before long, they are all confronted with the dilemma of who should move into the flat. With Nick away on a last-minute job, Sam offers to leave but Angie won't hear of it. She insists he stay and informs Daphne that she'll just have to share her "granny flat" with Sam.

The fate of having to share her living quarters with Sam is almost more than Daphne can bear. She is especially repulsed by Sam's taxidermy hobby and his growing collection of stuffed carcasses (the most prominent of which is a penguin). She never has anything remotely resembling a kind word for him. "I reckon she thinks I'm too thick to know when I'm being insulted," he says to Nick. Yet for some reason Sam himself can't explain, he is very much attracted to Daphne, and is determined to make a good impression on her. "Some men want to scale Everest, I want to scale Daphne." Daphne's refusal to see any of Sam's better qualities often comes across as cruel, but Sam is nonetheless willing to lick his wounds and try again.

Ensuing episodes center on their attempts to live together under one roof. As if Daphne's almost daily rejections of Sam's advances aren't enough, Sam must contend with a new neighbor, Major Giles Bradshaw—a prissy, retired Army officer whose archaic sense of manners and purple prose appeal to Daphne's idea of a gentleman. Giles and Sam are not destined to be friends. Things go wrong early on, however, when Giles invites Daphne to his place for a Chinese meal he claims to have prepared himself. His story is that he learned to cook while working undercover for the military in Red China. When Daphne later discovers white take-out cartons in Bradshaw's trash, she refuses to speak to him for days.

In "Arrivals and Departures," Giles is still pleading for forgiveness from Daphne. Her sense of betrayal has made her depressed, but a surprise visit from her attractive friend Camilla lifts her spirits. When Camilla first lays eyes on the disheveled Sam. Daphne's first instinct is to apologize for her flatmate, but Camilla is instantly turned on. "Lucky old Daphers," she murmurs to Sam. "You're quite a hunk, aren't you?" Despite being married (apparently to a cold fish of a husband), Camilla can't get her mind off Sam, and finds ways of sneaking into his bedroom when Daphne is otherwise occupied.

Sam has a tough time keeping Camilla at arm's length, explaining "I'm trying to keep myself pure for Daphne." He even tries telling Daphne that her friend practically attacked him, but Daphne, of course, can't comprehend such a thing, and dismisses the story as one of Sam's rants.

Giles arrives at the front door with flowers and an explanation that all he wanted to do with his fictional war stories was to impress her. Daphne finally forgives him. Later, she and Camilla go upstairs to babysit for Angie and Nick. Camilla leaves earlier than planned, in order to sneak back down to Sam's bedroom window. This time, Sam's resistance has run low, and he lets her in. When Daphne returns to the flat, Sam again tries to tell her that "She's in there on my bed, starkers, panting for me. Why can't you be more like her?" Daphne again rejects the idea and puts the milk bottles outside on the front landing. She catches Camilla backing halfway out of Sam's window. He pokes his head out and tells Daphne, "You'd better order an extra pint for me, Daphne. If Camilla's stopping on, I'm gonna need all my strength."

Angela Thorne as the strong-willed Daphne is barely recognizable to anyone who knows her primarily as the somewhat mousy and submissive Marjory in *To The Manor Born.* Here, she gives Penelope Keith a run for her money when it comes to portraying an overbearing, stuck-up snob.

Michael Elphick has kept busy since *Three Up, Two Down* as the star of a TV drama series *Boon* (which he worked on between series of *Three Up, Two Down*) and another drama series, *Harry.*

Lysette Anthony used *Three Up, Two Down* as a springboard for a successful acting and modeling career (which included a *Playboy* pictorial).

HOT METAL

LWT
1986-1988
12 Episodes

Written by Andrew Marshall and David Renwick
Produced by Humphrey Barclay

Cast:

HARRY STRINGER	Geoffrey Palmer
TERENCE "TWIGGY" RATHBONE	Robert Hardy
RUSSELL SPAM	Robert Hardy
RICHARD LIPTON	Richard Wilson (series 2)

Hot Metal is a scathing satire of London's infamous tabloid newspapers and their journalistic practices. While it is tricky to parody an institution that nearly parodies itself on a daily basis, *Hot Metal* goes gleefully over the top with its characters, plotlines, and pointed attitude towards Fleet Street's sheets.

The series opens as the failing newspaper *The Crucible* is bought by mogul Terence "Twiggy" Rathbone, president of Rathouse International and a shameless and tactless capitalist. He appoints the integrity-soaked Harry Stringer as his executive managing editor and promptly introduces him to his boss, Russell Spam. Russell not only shares Rathbone's vision of running a top-selling tabloid without regard to journalistic integrity, he is also a dead ringer for Rathbone (Robert Hardy, playing both roles, may be familiar to PBS viewers from his role in *All Creatures Great and Small*). The bombastic Russell rarely sits still and takes delight in easing Harry out the door in order to concentrate on creating blatantly fictitious and inflammatory headlines. Russell has no fear about possible recriminations by his newspaper's victims, including the royal family. "They can't sue us for publishing malicious rumors in good faith," he reasons.

A memorable scene occurs in this premiere episode. Since it is obvious that Harry's quest to maintain a respectful newspaper will forever clash with Russell's mad dog tactics, Russell assigns Harry to a "temporary" office until a proper space can be found. Where is Harry's new office? In the elevator. The shot of Harry sitting at his desk in the elevator, actually trying to do some work and answering the phone, as other building employees enter and exit at each floor serves as a perfect indication of the comic direction the series intends to take. In fact, before the first episode is over Harry discovers a note on Russell's calendar to write a "Royal Pregnancy" headline nine months in the future. How can Russell possibly know? Simple. The proud, slimy "ace" reporter Greg Kettle has tracked down Prince Andrew's latest flame in Switzerland. We witness Greg sneaking into her room to ever-so-daintily puncture her supply of condoms. While still in Switzerland, Greg also meets a mysterious old man who convincingly claims to be the exiled Soviet Premiere Nikita Khrushchev!

In the second series, Richard Wilson replaces Geoffrey Palmer. Wilson had appeared earlier in the feature film version of the television series

Whoops, Apocalypse written by Andrew Marshall and David Renwick. Renwick and Wilson later team up again for *One Foot in the Grave*.

Hot Metal producer Humphrey Barclay received praise from journalists at the time who knew from working for tabloid moguls Rupert Murdoch and Robert Maxwell how the exploits at the fictional tabloid *The Crucible* were only a half-step away from reality. Barclay said at the time, "They tell me it's so far-fetched it's impossible to imagine that anything could top it—except that Murdoch and Maxwell manage to do it every day."

EXECUTIVE STRESS

Thames TV
1986, 1989
19 Episodes

Written by George Layton
Directed and produced by John Howard
    Davies

Cast:

DONALD FAIRCHILD	Geoffrey Palmer (series 1)
	Peter Bowles (series 2, 3)
CAROLINE FAIRCHILD	Penelope Keith
EDGAR FRANKLAND	Harry Ditson
ANTHEA DUXBURY	Elizabeth Counsell

Executive Stress was the second series created and written by George Layton. Set in the world of publishing, it brought back popular sitcom stars Penelope Keith and Geoffrey Palmer as a married couple with a secret: they're married. The premiere episode cleverly establishes their dilemma, and whets the appetite for how they will cope with it.

When we first meet the Fairchilds, Donald is a managing editor for Ginsberg Publishing, a drab, out-of-touch company led by the elderly Herman Ginsberg. Donald expects Ginsberg to announce his retirement soon so he can take over as managing director. Caroline, having long ago put her own publishing career on hold to raise their children, has seen the last of the offspring leave the nest and informs Donald she intends to resume her career. He doesn't take the idea very seriously, which makes her even more determined to find a job. While waiting in the reception area for an interview at Oasis Publishing (where she uses her maiden name, Fielding), she runs into Anthea, her former secretary, who sings her praises to the company's personnel director. Caroline of course gets the job.

The next day, Ginsberg surprises everyone by announcing that Edgar Franklin, an American, will lead Oasis Publishing's takeover of Ginsberg

Publishing. Donald is hurt at first, convinced he's losing out on his advancement, but Edgar wants him to stay on after the takeover to be the sales and marketing director. He even gives Donald a personal tour of Oasis and introduces him to several staff members. Edgar then opens the office door of the new Editorial Director, Caroline Fielding. Unknown to Edgar, introductions are hardly necessary. Donald and Caroline both register shock for a second or two, but each manages to keep a straight face through the introductions.

The situation gets stickier when it is casually mentioned at an executive meeting that Oasis policy forbids married couples from working together. Donald later tells Caroline that one of them will have to leave, and it isn't going to be *him*, but Caroline stands firm and refuses to give up her new position. The frustrated Donald concedes that they'll just have to be especially careful not to let it slip that they're married. His paranoia takes hold quickly, though. When Anthea joins them on the commuter train home, he panics and gets off at a stop miles out of his way to avoid any suspicion. Caroline has to pick him up at their real train stop hours later. Donald's strategy obviously has a few kinks to be worked out.

Despite the program's early success, Geoffrey Palmer abruptly left *Executive Stress* after the first series, much to the consternation of George Layton. "I actually wrote the part for Geoffrey Palmer," he explained, "and at the time Penelope Keith was a top TV star. I don't think he realized that he had the best part. He just made a career decision because he felt he was overexposed in comedy, so he dropped out. At the time I was furious because he could have made that decision before he'd done the series. Anyway it did go on, and it was all right."

In fact, when Palmer left, the series was close to being canceled. Peter Bowles continues the story.

> I was having a social conversation with Penelope Keith on the telephone. And she told me that she was very worried that because Geoffrey Palmer left the series of what was going to happen to it. She was just speaking on a personal level. And I said, 'Well, is it a part I could play?' And she said, 'Yes, it is.' And I said, 'Well, all right, I'll do it.' And she said, 'Are you serious?' And I said, 'Yes, of course I'm serious.' So, within about an hour, they phoned me from the television company, and within another hour they had the scripts sent around to me by motorbike. The next day [George Layton] came to see me, and within two or three days I was signed up to do it. I was only a bit miffed they hadn't asked me in the first place!

In fact, Peter Bowles would have been an excellent choice to take over the role of Donald anyway, even if he hadn't thought of it himself. Joining the show enabled him to reunite with Penelope Keith, his former co-star of *To the Manor Born*. There was naturally much hype accompanying their appearance together on yet another hit series. (Geoffrey Palmer, curiously enough, has continued his sitcom work—most notably with five series of *As Time Goes By*, co-starring Judi Dench.)

In a pivotal *Executive Stress* episode, Edgar, who is aware of the Fairchilds' marriage after overhearing a conversation between them, decides to have some fun as he puts the couple to the test. Since Caroline's husband is supposedly on long-term assignment in Saudi Arabia, Edgar tells Caroline that she will be the new head of Oasis Publishing in Jedda. Finding herself trapped by her own deception, Caroline decides to resign from the firm, fumbling for the excuse that her husband has been sent back to England. Edgar asks her to hold off on her decision until after the next executive meeting. There, he announces that he wants Caroline and Donald to become comanaging directors after Edgar returns to the United States to take over his father's duties. He also announces that Caroline and Donald are indeed married, but they're too good to let go because of an outdated company rule (instituted by Edgar's father to keep Edgar's mother from working in the office). Caroline and Donald's challenge of keeping their marriage a secret is soon replaced by that of having to share the responsibilities and authority equally.

The program ran for three series altogether, but Layton feels it could have had an even longer life. "Three series isn't bad," he said, "but it could easily have gone on for more."

THE TWO OF US

LWT
1986–1990
29 Episodes

Written by Alex Shearer
Produced by Marcus Plantin, Robin Carr

Cast:

ASHLEY . . . . Nicholas Lyndhurst
ELAINE . . . . Janet Dibley
PERCE . . . . Patrick Troughton (later Tenniel Evans)

This breezy comedy, which has been likened to the American *Mad about You* (although this series came first), follows the romance of young, attractive lovers Ashley Philips and Elaine Walker. While they have fallen into a cozy arrangement by living together, it is Ashley, in a bit of a role reversal from the stereotypical set-up, who wants to get married and start a family, and Elaine who resists. However, they manage to put the issue on the back burner while dealing with the more immediate matters of their daily lives.

The episode "Comparisons" opens with Ashley and Elaine undecided about how to spend their Saturday night. Ashley is content to maintain the routine of going down to the local pub to meet their friends, but Elaine wants a change of pace and a chance to meet new people. They decide to invite the couple upstairs, Matthew and Nicole, over for an evening of chatting and Trivial Pursuit. Ashley's assessment of the couple as materialistic yuppies seems on the mark, but Elaine, happy to make new friends and eager to impress them, manages to find a few things in common with them. Ashley, sneering at Matthew and Nicole's upwardly-mobile airs, quickly becomes the odd man out. "So what if they are upwardly mobile?" Elaine argues later that night, "What are we? We just seem to be horizontally stag-

nant." She adds that expanding their horizons is necessary for development and growth, but Ashley will have none of it.

As Elaine spends more time (and money) with Nicole, Ashley begins to tire of their new friends' yuppie influence, and fears that Elaine will continue to spend more money than their budget will allow. Much to his relief, however, Matthew and Nicole have decided to move out of the building and into a larger flat. Not only that, but they've begun to make suspicious excuses to get out of plans for future get-togethers. "They've moved on to more useful people," Ashley concludes. He and Elaine later apologize to each other, agreeing that they are happy even without high incomes and material frills. Just then, the new neighbors stop by. They're a pleasant young couple, if a tad nerdy, and are immediately impressed with Ashley and Elaine's apartment, choice of clothes, and just about everything else. A smug Ashley finds himself on the flip side of the coin at last.

Patrick Troughton, who played Ashley's youthful grandfather Perce (until his death in 1987), was perhaps better known to sci-fi buffs as the second Dr. Who.

RED DWARF

BBC-2
1988-1993, 1997-
52 Episodes
3 Specials

The crew of Red Dwarf (*left to right*): Cat (Danny John-Jules), Kris Kochanski (Chloe Annett), Kryten (Robert Llewellyn), Rimmer (Chris Barrie), and Lister (Craig Charles). *BBC Worldwide*

Written by Rob Grant and Doug Naylor
Produced by Paul Jackson

Available on home video in the U.S.

Cast:

DAVE LISTER	Craig Charles
ARNOLD RIMMER	Chris Barrie
KRYTEN	Robert Llewellyn
CAT	Danny John-Jules
HOLLY	Norman Lovett (series 1, 2)
	Hattie Hayridge (series 3-7)
KRISTINE KOCHANSKI	Chloe Annett (series 7, 8)

Red Dwarf has been hailed in both Britain and America as one of the most imaginative sitcoms ever to appear on television. It stands out for several reasons, not the least of which is that it belongs to the sparsely populated genre of the science fiction sitcom, a true rarity for British as well as American television. One American series that attempted such a mix was *Quark* starring Richard Benjamin in 1978. The network programming strategy at that time was to capitalize on the *Star Wars* craze, so the show placed its characters on a garbage-collecting spacecraft. *Quark* lasted less than three months. No series from *Mork and Mindy* to *Third Rock from the Sun* has had any true sci-fi elements.

Red Dwarf has become a major cult favorite not only among Britcom fans, but among science fiction fans as well. The plots are sometimes mind-boggling but no less plausible than those on any of the *Star Trek* series, and the use of impressive special effects enables *Red Dwarf* to create suspenseful

as well as comic moments. One of the strongest and most important attributes of the series lies with some truly interesting characters who, beyond the jokes, are capable of revealing their fears, hopes, and dreams with a surprising regularity. It helps that the cast has great chemistry.

Red Dwarf creators Rob Grant and Doug Naylor honed their writing skills on several TV sketch comedies such as the BBC's popular *Splitting Image* while working their way to creating their own sitcom. Grant was especially interested in science fiction. Their *Red Dwarf* pilot script was based on a sketch they had written earlier for a radio series, *Son of Cliche*. The sketch was called "Dave Hollins, Space Cadet." Grant and Naylor's excitement over their pilot TV script was tempered by the BBC's reluctance to pursue the project. Producer Paul Jackson supported the team but remained pessimistic about the show's chances. He decided to send the script to BBC Manchester, where Commissioning Editor Peter Risdale-Scott surprised them all by expressing his enthusiasm. *Red Dwarf* was given a fighting chance.

In the opening episode entitled "The End," we find David Lister on the immense Red Dwarf spaceship in the twenty-fourth century, where his job as maintenance man involves repairing such delicate equipment as the chicken soup dispensing machine. His bunkmate and immediate superior is Arnold Rimmer, a rather disagreeable chap whose attempts to climb the ladder of success invariably get him nowhere.

Rimmer commits the ultimate faux pas by allowing a radiation leak to kill 169 crew members, including himself. Only Lister survives. Just before the accident, Lister had been sent to the ship's suspended animation chamber for eighteen months as punishment for refusing to relinquish his pet cat (which, as a superior tells him, could be a disease carrier and isn't allowed on board). The ship's computer, Holly, who has an IQ of several thousand and appears as a human face on the ship's video screens, brings Lister out of his suspended state when the radiation levels become safe. The only catch is that three million years have gone by. Lister "awakens" to find himself alone, or so it appears at first. Holly has resurrected Rimmer as a hologram, although Rimmer wouldn't have been Lister's first choice or last choice to have as company. They later run into a most unexpected companion: Lister's own pet cat, protected from the radiation leak, produced the first of thousands of generations of descendants. Evolution eventually produced Cat, a vain, preening fashion plate who resembles James Brown with fangs and is always the first to seek a good hiding place in the face of danger.

While Grant and Naylor were at first timid to exploit the sci-fi aspects of the series, they quickly realized how many story possibilities could arise from the series' setting and characters. They allowed their imaginations to take off, which produced more complex stories and enabled the use of more elaborate special effects.

At the beginning of the second series, the crew comes upon a stranded android named Kryten, who later becomes a regular character in the third series. Kryten's superior artificial intelligence and problem-solving skills often collide with his more human-like foibles. The result is a cross between a robotic scientist and a pesky party guest. From this point on, the program's stories become more ambitious, and bizarre encounters with strange aliens are soon the norm.

Grant and Naylor became the series producers at the beginning of the third series, and used their expanded influence to make more changes. Norman Lovett as Holly left the show due to a contract dispute. Comedian Hattie Hayridge took over the role, thus giving Holly a new gender and platinum blonde bangs. The addition of Hayridge completed the longest-running incarnation of the cast (she had appeared in an earlier episode, "Parallel Universe," as Hilly, a computer counterpart to Red Dwarf's Holly).

"Backwards" is a particularly inspired episode, making brilliant use of video tricks to enhance the intricate details of the storyline. It opens with Lister and Cat engrossed in a *Flintstones* episode. "I think Wilma's sexy," Lister confesses. He and Cat trade observations about Wilma and Betty Rubble's desirable attributes. Meanwhile, Rimmer is administering Kryten's driving test aboard Starbug 1. The nervous Kryten accidentally ejects Rimmer out of his seat before they begin the test and proceed into space. Soon they find themselves entering a time hole and arrive back on Earth, where Starbug plunges in the middle of a pond. "I suppose you're going to fail me for this," ventures Kryten. Upon exploring the area, they find a road marker printed backwards and then hop a ride with a truck driver who "arrives" in reverse, speaks backwards, and takes them to Nodnol (London). Holly surmises that they've arrived on Earth during the Big Crunch, when the universe has stopped expanding and has begun to contract. Time itself, she reasons, has begun to move backwards as well. Rimmer decides that while they wait for the others to rescue them, he and Kryten might as well find jobs to fit in with the truly backward society. They find a theatrical agent's newspaper ad looking for a novelty act, and decide that everything they do naturally could now be considered a novelty.

After weeks of searching for their companions, Lister and Cat find the same time hole and land by the submerged Starbug. They soon find posters for Rimmer and Kryten's stage act, but the confusing language leads Lister to conclude that they're in Bulgaria. They make their way to the pub to watch their friends performing in glittery suits as the Reverse Brothers. Kryten's big finish is simply drinking a glass of water, much to the delight of the crowd. "The Bulgarians have very simple tastes," Lister explains. Soon, however, he figures out what's really going on. Surprisingly, Rimmer and Kryten have adjusted to the backwards life and feel no desire to leave. There's no death or crime here, Kryten explains. "Our first night here a mugger jumped us and forced fifty pounds inside my pocket!" But soon they are involved in a barroom brawl in which the room is actually straightened up as the brawl proceeds. Rimmer and Kryten eventually have a change of heart and return to the ship with Lister and Cat. As they exit the cab, the driver gives Lister a handful of money, plus a tip!

"Terrorform" provides an excellent example of how writers Grant and Naylor combine a sci-fi premise with a closer look inside one of their regular characters. The crew searches for crash victim Rimmer on a psi-moon, an artificial planetoid. "It tunes into an individual's psyche and adapts its terrain to mimic his mental state," explains Kryten. In other words, they are traveling through Rimmer's mind, and it's not a pleasant sight. All of his fears, neuroses, and personal demons have taken physical form. "This sounds like a twelve-change-of-underwear trip," Cat observes. They make their way through deep recesses such as the Swamp of Despair, where they find gravestones with epitaphs such as "Here lies self-respect, died age 24."

In 1992, Hollywood producer Linwood Boomer, a big fan of the show, proposed an American version of *Red Dwarf*. He intended to use a mostly American cast but also asked Robert Llewellyn to continue his role as Kryten in the new version (Terry Farrell, later of *Star Trek: Deep Space Nine* was cast as Cat, and Jane Leeves, later of *Frasier*, was to be the new Holly). Grant and Naylor flew to Hollywood to serve as consultants, but soon found themselves rewriting an unsatisfactory pilot script. Other setbacks and a general apathy among network executives brought the project to a halt. *Red Dwarf* had become the latest casualty in a long line of Britcoms to suffer from attempts by American television executives to duplicate or Americanize the original hits.

Back in Britain, the show began a tumultuous period behind the scenes. Director Ed Bye had agreed to direct *The Ruby Wax Show*, whose taping schedule conflicted with that of *Red Dwarf*. Wax, an American comedian and talk show host, happens to be Mrs. Ed Bye, so her influence in his decision to direct her show was no doubt significant. *Red Dwarf*'s replacements for Bye didn't work out, so Grant and Naylor eventually took over the directing reins themselves.

The sixth series begins with a major change in the storyline. In "Psirens," Lister awakens after a 200-year sleep, and suffers some temporary amnesia. Rimmer has been off-line as well, until Kryten re-activates him, and then debriefs the crew. Red Dwarf has been stolen by unknown thieves, leaving the Dwarfers to chase after it in Starbug.

Without the Red Dwarf around, there could be no Holly. This development required the dismissal of Hattie Hayridge as Holly. Another important story development took place in the episode "Legion," in which a strange but seemingly friendly being permanently converts Rimmer from a soft light hologram to hard light, giving him solid form and enabling him to touch.

Much of the sixth series was rushed into production when the BBC condensed the shooting schedule. The actors found little time to memorize their lines and found themselves having to read from teleprompters. Unable to maintain such a hectic pace, the series closed production at the end of that series. *Red Dwarf VI* is nonetheless often considered the best of the series, and achieved top ratings on BBC-2. It also won the 1994 BBC British Comedy Award, and the 1994 International Emmy.

After a three-year gap, during which time Rob Grant and Doug Naylor ended their partnership, *Red Dwarf VII* arrived on British screens with eight episodes in January of 1997. Doug Naylor stayed with the series, and hired additional writers to lessen his workload. Ed Bye returned as director and made the big step of continuing production without a studio audience. This greatly relieved a lot of the stress the cast had come to expect during the studio tapings of the previous series. (From this point on, a studio audience would be brought in only to view the finished product, and have its laughter recorded and added to the soundtrack.) The loss of the audience also

The crew takes a ride through "The Rimmer Experience," devised by Kryten in the Artificial Reality suite. *BBC Worldwide*

allowed for larger sets and more flexibility in the shooting schedule. Bye expressed some concern, however, that the absence of the audience might throw off the actors' performances. "They have an invisible communication with an audience," he said. "It's difficult for the performers, who've got to imagine these people laughing . . . whenever I shoot without an audience there, I leave a space for the audience to laugh, but I never leave long enough. It's very difficult to shoot with dead air." Still, the cast members' long experience with each other helped smooth the transition, as did Bye's experience of directing series such as *The Detectives* without a studio audience. *Red Dwarf* was also now shot on film rather than videotape. That plus additional location shoots gave the series the more polished look of a feature film.

Another change during *Red Dwarf VII* came with the decision to add a female member to the crew. Chloe Annett as Kristine Kochanski, Lister's ex-girlfriend, proved a wonderful choice. Annett's presence (beginning with the episode "Ouroboros") provided balance for the reduced role of Rimmer, since Chris Barrie agreed to return for only a limited number of episodes. The

episodes and high ratings gave the cast and crew a renewed enthusiasm to continue the series.

On February 14th, 1998, the BBC devoted an entire evening's programming to the tenth anniversary of *Red Dwarf*. Production on *Red Dwarf VIII* began in the summer of 1998, with Chris Barrie (and Norman Lovett, the original Holly) back full-time.

Red Dwarf VIII opens with the Red Dwarf and its crew newly resurrected by the nanobots. Rimmer also enjoys a new lease on life since he has technically been dead since the premiere episode. Our heroes, however, have been arrested for stealing Starbug, and have to serve their sentences in the penitentiary. For this series, side trips to various planets are kept to a minimum, as most of the action is confined to the ship's cavernous prison. Lister and Rimmer are bunkmates once again (allowing for scenes reminiscent of the program's early days), and Kryten has been designated a woman and must live with Kristine and the female prisoners.

The ever-evolving nature of *Red Dwarf*, from that of sitcom to sci-fi adventure with laughs, allows for still more changes to take place in series 8. The studio audience has been brought back much to the delight of the cast, who realized after the previous series how important it is to hear a live audience react to the comedy. Chris Barrie, Craig Charles, and the others almost surprised themselves with their optimism for the series' future. "It's great to have Norman back," Barrie said in a magazine interview, "Chloe is excellent, and the boys are the boys, and we're all happy."

The program has become the most successful comedy on BBC-2. A full-length feature film version of the series will be shot in 2000.

The bouncy *Red Dwarf* theme was written by Howard Goodall, and is sung with great vigor over the closing credits by actress Jenna Russell. It was released as a single in Britain.

Colin's Sandwich

BBC
1988–1990
12 Episodes

Jen (Louisa Rix) and Colin (Mel Smith). *BBC Worldwide*

Written by Paul Smith and Terry Kyan
Produced by John Kilby

Cast:

Colin Watkins . . . . Mel Smith
Jenny . . . . Louisa Rix
Des . . . . Mike Grady

Mel Smith and his comedy partner Griff Rhys-Jones have been longtime favorites with British audiences due to their work on *Not the Nine O'Clock News* and later on their own series, *Alas Smith and Jones*. In *Colin's Sandwich*, Mel Smith tests the sitcom waters and comes up with a short-lived but very funny series.

Smith plays Colin Watkins, a struggling writer of suspense and horror stories. He has the thankless day job of working for British Rail's public relations department, where he must suffer complaints of all kinds by disgruntled commuters. Once he retreats to his typewriter though, he loses himself in the gruesome stories that bubble up in his mind.

It is when Colin has to deal with the real world that he begins to lose his grip. Although he's an intelligent fellow, he is also an insecure, self-conscious, and hopelessly neurotic worrywart.

Throughout the series, he tortures himself by predicting doom at the outset of each task he undertakes. Hence, he becomes a master of self-fulfilling prophecy, and inevitably becomes panic-stricken when a real or imagined disaster appears imminent. Miraculously, he is supported by his beautiful and ever-patient girlfriend Jen. She is everything Colin is not—poised, sensible, and calm. They're not much for open displays of affection for each other, but there's obviously something keeping them together. Besides, who else but Jen would pick up the pieces in the wake of Colin's self-destructive tirades?

Mel Smith makes the most of the character, and is at his best when he's throwing himself into histrionics over the most trivial matters. In one episode, Colin's nerves are put to the test when he is asked to be best man at coworker Trevor's wedding. Colin dreads the idea and nearly tries to back out, until he decides that he could probably offer a few creative variations on the traditional best man duties. He is in no way prepared for all of the responsibilities Trevor heaps upon him. When he presents his prepared speech to Jen the next day, which consists of supposed love letters between Trevor and the bride-to-be, Jen appears unmoved by the comedy routine. Colin panics, but she assures him that it's funny and he should keep it.

Colin's idea to hold a classy bachelor party at a Chinese restaurant bombs when the bored guests do little more than stare at each other in the empty restaurant. He gives in and invites them all back to his apartment for an evening of drunken debauchery. After thoroughly cleaning up the flat, he suddenly discovers that Trevor's wedding ring, which Colin has been holding for safekeeping, is missing. In a hilarious scene, Jen arrives the next morning to find the entire apartment ransacked. She finds Colin sitting amid the mess in the living room. He's bleary-eyed, exhausted, and barely has the strength to speak, but feebly shows Jen how the missing ring has been hanging from his neck all along. His troubles are far from over when his speech at the wedding reception does indeed fall flat with the guests. This finally causes him to snap, as he launches into a rambling tirade of insults that grind the joyous proceedings to a halt. Colin awakens later on his couch, relieved that the whole dreaded ordeal was just a dream. Jen is seated beside him to reassure him, "No, it wasn't."

MAY TO DECEMBER

BBC
1989-1994
41 Episodes

Written by Paul A. Mendelson
Produced by Sydney Lotterby

Cast:

ALEC CALLENDAR	Anton Rodgers
ZOE ANGEL	Eve Matheson (later Leslie Dunlop)
MISS FLOOD	Frances White
HILARY	Rebecca Lacey
JAIME	Paul Venables
SIMONE	Carolyn Pickles

Love at first sight: Zoe (Eve Matheson) and Alec (Anton Rodgers). *BBC Worldwide*

This series explores the ups and downs of a May-December romance with humor and honesty as it rises above the clichéd jokes about the age difference between the two main characters.

Alec Callendar is a proud Scotsman and founding partner of a modest but successful law firm specializing in divorces, wills, etc. He is a widower in his early fifties with two grown children, Jaime and Simone. One day he is called upon to help a pretty but unhappy young woman, Zoe Angel, a gym teacher who is divorcing her unfaithful husband. Although he deals with his new client in a businesslike way, Alec notices his heart beating just a bit faster whenever Zoe arrives for an appointment. She is shy and self-effacing, and uses her charming sense of humor to help deal with the trauma of becoming a twenty-seven-year-old divorcee. Alec soon finds it difficult to get her out of his mind. Lucky for him, the feeling is mutual.

Before long, Alec and Zoe discover that their romance is not an easy one to nurture. They have

no doubts about their feelings for each other, but they are painfully aware of the outside obstacles to overcome. They have to endure long looks from strangers in restaurants, not to mention the reactions of their respective family members. Alec's prudish daughter Simone, a vicar's wife with her nose in a chronically upturned position, is horrified to see her father dating a woman twenty-five years younger than he. The time-honored rituals such as introducing each other to their respective families take on new dimensions and added stress. In one episode, Zoe's parents, initially a bit chilly toward Alec, find themselves reminiscing with him about days long gone by. The only problem is that Zoe is too young to share their memories, and can't get a word in edgewise.

The storyline evolves steadily throughout the series' run. Alec and Zoe eventually get married and begin planning a family of their own. However, Zoe suffers a miscarriage, which hits both of them hard. In the following series, however, Zoe has a baby girl who is named Fleur. Alec loves showing off the baby to admiring passersby, but isn't happy about being mistaken for the grandfather. The new family moves to a "neutral" home, which just happens to be across the street from Simone.

A good deal of the action takes place in the law office, and features the wonderfully airheaded secretary Hilary. Always sweet and soft-spoken, even when inadvertently tossing sharp verbal barbs, much of Hilary's charm lies in the fact that she's totally unaware of how her observations and comments border on insult. She also speaks often of her boyfriend Derek, who tends to spend most of his time incarcerated for various scrapes with the law. Alec's longtime secretary Miss Flood is prim and proper on the surface but also has a sentimental streak and is very loyal to Alec. She provides a nice balance to the flighty Hilary. Miss Flood eventually marries but stays with the firm. Paul Venables's role as Jaime grows as he becomes a law partner with his father.

There were several cast changes throughout the show's run. Clive Francis as Alec's law partner Miles Henty left the series fairly early in its run but soon afterward co-starred with Nicholas Lyndhurst in *The Piglet Files.* The most significant cast change was that of Leslie Dunlop replacing Eve Matheson as Zoe. Whereas Matheson played Zoe as somewhat fragile and unsure of herself, Dunlop played her as a woman with more self-confidence and assertiveness. Rebecca Lacey as Hilary left the show late in its run, and was replaced by Ashley Jensen as Rosie, a loud, Scottish whirlwind of energy.

PART III

"I don't believe it!..."
Britcoms of the 1990s

BRITISH TV IN THE 1990S

As the decade opened, British television saw Rupert
Murdoch's Sky Broadcasting eventually absorb its
rival British Satellite Broadcasting. The result,
called BSkyB, offered six channels of movies,
twenty-four-hour news, entertainment, and sports.
Channel 5 would join the increasingly heavy
over-the-air competition in 1997.
The Broadcasting Act of 1991 required the
fifteen regional ITV franchises to offer bids for
renewed licenses. The process caused great
upheaval among the broadcasting companies.
Yorkshire Television bid almost thirty-eight million
pounds and later merged with Tyne Tees. Thames
TV, however, found itself outbid, as did TV-am,
producer of morning breakfast shows. Thames was
replaced by Carlton, and TV-am bowed to Good
Morning Television (GMTV). However, while
Thames lost its broadcast franchise, it has survived
as an independent production company, able to sell

its product to any channel. The Broadcasting Act also required both the BBC and ITV to purchase 25 percent of their programming from independent producers. This provided a great opportunity for existing and new production companies to work in cooperation with the BBC to create new programming. Two such companies, Tiger Television and Aspect Films, merged in 1993 to form Tiger Aspect Productions (the producer of *The Vicar of Dibley*). Theatre of Comedy Productions has brought us *As Time Goes By*, and comedian Lenny Henry's own company, Crucial Films Productions, produced his sitcom *Chef!*.

Hat Trick Productions is one independent production company that has thrived throughout the 1980s and 1990s without relying on the BBC as a customer. Formed in the early 1980s by comedy writer/producers Rory McGrath, Jimmy Mulville, and producer Denise O'Donoghue, Hat Trick quickly made a name for itself by supplying ITV and Channel 4 with a fresh comedy style in its programs. The most successful of these have been *Drop the Dead Donkey* and the improvisational series *Whose Line Is It, Anyway?* (the American version, hosted by Drew Carey, was successfully launched on ABC in 1998). As the company's reputation as a haven for new ideas has grown, so has its stable of top-notch writers and performers.

The 1990s saw a continuation of both conventional and innovative situation comedies appealing to British and American viewers. The full spectrum of comic scenarios and styles, as seen in the following section, is quite remarkable.

Once considered on the cutting edge of comedy, most of the alternative writer/performers of the mid-1980s are finding themselves on the cusp of middle-age. Consequently, their styles in some cases may be mellowing a bit with them (although Jennifer Saunders's *Absolutely Fabulous* is never likely to be described as "mellow"). It is inevitable that the comedy rebels of the mid-1980s would now begin to see a still younger generation of comedians run rampant, mostly on Britain's late night programs. Names such as Harry Enfield and the team of Vic Reeves and Bob Mortimer are not familiar to Americans yet. However, if the successes of their predecessors are any indication, it is merely a matter of time before the younger generation takes to the sitcom genre, and tries its hand at making Americans laugh.

ONE FOOT IN THE GRAVE

BBC-1

1990-1995
30 Episodes, 7 Specials

Written by David Renwick
Directed and produced by Susan Belbin

Available on home video in the U.S.

Cast:

VICTOR MELDREW	Richard Wilson
MARGARET MELDREW	Annette Crosbie
MRS. WARBOYS	Doreen Mantle
PATRICK	Angus Deayton
PIPPA	Janine Duvitski
NICK SWAINEY	Owen Brenman

Par for the course: Pippa (Janine Duvitski) and Patrick (Angus Deayton) look on as Victor (Richard Wilson) and Margaret (Annette Crosbie) deal with a tree growing inside their car.
BBC Worldwide

One Foot in the Grave has been the recipient of over a dozen major awards and praise both from the viewing public and from those in the British television industry. The simple premise of a couple coping with late middle-age blooms into a unique series in which they find themselves in the most absurd, even macabre, comic situations. Several of these situations enable the program to push the boundaries of the sitcom form itself.

Sixty-year-old Victor Meldrew has not taken kindly to impending senior citizenship. While he seems destined to live out his life as an old curmudgeon, we get the impression that he was a young curmudgeon as well.

Victor is perpetually at the losing end of his war with the world. As the series opens, he is given an early retirement from his job as a security officer. The loss of his job comes as a shock, leaving him without a clue as to what he should now do with himself. With so much time on his hands, he reveals a knack for finding trouble simply by puttering around the house, going on errands, and dealing with those in various service industries. As played to cranky perfection by Richard Wilson,

Victor is often astounded by how the twists of fate can so easily turn his life upside down. Upon witnessing the latest calamity, he is usually left to gasp, "I don't believe it!"

Victor's sad-eyed wife Margaret tolerates her grouchy husband as best she can, but often forsakes her calm exterior by giving him a good dressing-down when he commits a major botch-up. He is forever a source of consternation to her, but despite the occasional temptation to leave him to wallow in his misanthropy, she accepts her lot in life, and can't deny her love for him.

Victor is more than a stereotypical sitcom grouch. He's not really a nasty or unpleasant man, but appears so only in self-defense, whenever life decides to kick him around a little. His methods of retaliation often backfire though, leaving him to later truly regret his harsh words or actions. He is also given to introspective moments that leave him contemplating life and what it all means in the end. Series director Susan Belbin proudly describes the show as one without gimmicks. "This was just a guy who was retired early and became aware of everyday life," she said, "which none of us are quite aware of in the same way until you've got time on your hands. I kind of tried to shoot it like that, sort of wide so there would be empty spaces around him [to show] the loneliness of the situation and frustrations of everyday life."

Richard Wilson was creator/writer David Renwick's first choice to play Victor Meldrew, but he initially turned down the part. The search for a second choice proved fruitless, and after a bit of good-natured arm twisting, Wilson admitted that the scripts were indeed quite good. According to Renwick, *One Foot in the Grave* began production rather hastily. Renwick submitted the pilot episode in January of 1989. After months of deliberations the BBC commissioned the second episode, but within a space of another few weeks the series was in full production. The reason for the sudden burst of progress was that another series had fallen through, leaving *One Foot* to inherit another program's production date and broadcast date. So, instead of following the usual hurry-up-and-wait scenario, it was more a matter of wait-and-hurry-up.

An outstanding episode from the second series, "Who Will Buy?," is so perfectly constructed that aspiring comedy writers can either attempt to emulate it or simply switch off their laptops in surrender. The episode deserves a lengthy synopsis here (although it can be even better appreciated on video).

As is typical of most *One Foot* episodes, "Who Will Buy?" opens with seemingly unrelated and unimportant remarks and actions that only come into play much later in the story. Victor and Margaret are watching a tape of a TV murder mystery that ends with the victim clutching a sprig of basil in his hand, implicating a character named Basil as the murderer. Victor complains about getting pimples on his nose, probably due to the Smarties candies he gulps down in bulk. He and Margaret watch TV accompanied by Victor's ventriloquist doll he has recently dusted off to practice with in his idle hours, but the dummy gives Margaret the creeps, and she banishes it to the downstairs bathroom.

The next day, after slamming the door on a salesman pitching toy dinosaurs, Victor chats with neighbor Nick Swainey in the backyard. Nick is organizing an amateur night for the old-age pensioner's charity he works for, and persuades Victor to perform his ventriloquist act. Meanwhile, Margaret, making a delivery for her florist shop, has mistakenly knocked on the door of an elderly blind man, Albert,

who initially mistakes her for the locksmith who is due to secure his apartment. Margaret stumbles a bit through the darkened flat (Albert doesn't need lights), and knocks over his dominoes set. She then performs a good deed by reading a letter Albert believes was sent from his son and grandchildren in Australia. There is no such letter, only junk mail, so Margaret "reads" a heartwarming letter she concocts spontaneously. Albert says he must think of a nice Christmas present to send to his grandchildren.

Victor, meanwhile, is in his living room awkwardly chatting with a friendly young couple, Patrick and Pippa, who have arrived with several suitcases. When Margaret arrives, he ushers her into the kitchen. "Who are they?" she asks. "I don't know!" he answers. Wracking their brains, neither of them can figure out who their guests are. Assuming they must be relatives, Victor insists on bringing their luggage up to the guest room. Patrick and Pippa would rather leave. Margaret, with a sudden realization, sees them off before explaining to Victor that the couple in fact live right next door—they had briefly said hello while leaving on a month's vacation the day Victor and Margaret moved in! In later episodes, Victor's relationship with next-door neighbor Patrick degenerates into a running feud. Patrick is played by Angus Deayton, host of the popular satire/quiz show *Have I Got News for You*. Patrick's wife Pippa is played by Janine Duvitski, also known as Jane in *Waiting for God*.

The next day, Victor, annoyed about the two prominent pimples on his nose, performs his ventriloquist act at the charity show, which is otherwise cluttered with heavy metal rock groups. Margaret arrives at Albert's flat to visit, but finds the front door ominously ajar. Later, Nick Swainey receives a call backstage informing him that Albert, regularly visited by the pensioner's charity, was murdered in his apartment. When Pippa, as a favor to Margaret, arrives to pick up Victor, Nick explains to her that Albert was found clutching a two-dot domino in his hand. She thinks back to the clue in the TV murder mystery, then happens to spot Victor (and his two pimples) backstage, pulling off his dummy's head. They arrive back home, where Victor hands a nervous Pippa the dummy and says, "He goes in the downstairs toilet. Could you be quick, please, I think he's bursting." Victor and Margaret look on in bewilderment as Pippa holds the dummy up in front of the toilet, as if assisting a small child.

Margaret and her neighbors later discuss how Albert was to have new locks put on his front door, but he canceled the appointment. He needed money for something else. What could have been so important to him? The closing shot is a high-angle of a postal delivery truck leaving behind a box at Albert's door. A long, slow zoom reveals the label on the box to be that of the toy dinosaur company. It is the final irony in an episode so complex and full of loose threads.

"Monday Morning Will Be Fine," an episode from the third series, opens with Victor using a neighbor's phone across the street to inform the police that the Meldrews' house has been robbed clean. The neighbors admit, with surprising calm, that they in fact assisted the burglars and offered them a tea break, unaware that they were removing the Meldrews' furniture without permission. Victor is speechless. He returns home to sit with Margaret in their empty living room. They soon miss the television most of all.

They find refuge from this latest setback down at the pub, where an old classmate of Victor's spots him and invites him for a drink. He reminisces about the old days, and about a "real prat" named Victor Meldrew. "You remember him, Steve," he says to Victor. "He was a right bastard." The case of mistaken identity grows even less flattering to Victor as the conversation continues. Elsewhere in the pub, Margaret runs into a work colleague to whom she had earlier given a phony excuse for not attending her daughter's wedding. Margaret's husband, according to her story, is in the hospital. But within minutes she and Victor are "introduced" to each other by their friends, and have to carry on the conversation as if they had just met. Later, the friends offer them a lift to their respective homes. Victor, who's now in too deep to say anything, must pick a house at random to be dropped off (in the rain). He reluctantly gets out of the car and heads toward the house, waiting for the others to drive off. They don't, preferring to wait until he actually gets inside the house. More complications follow, as is the norm in Victor's world.

Among the most memorable of David Renwick's outstanding scripts were those that took drastic diversions from the familiar sitcom format.

One such episode, "Timeless Time," takes place entirely in the Meldrews' bedroom late at night. Victor can't sleep, and before long, neither can

Margaret. Victor's malfunctioning car alarm soon awakens the rest of the neighborhood as well. After venturing outside to manually turn off the alarm, he returns to the bedroom, where a horrified Margaret blurts out that Victor's foot is not wedged in his slipper, but is instead stuck inside a dead hedgehog! Victor looks down to discover she's right. The comic antics give way at one point to a particularly poignant but brief discussion about their son, who died as an infant many years before. This revelation comes as a surprise to us but the couple does not dwell on it for long. Rather, the moment provides just a bit more insight into who Victor and Margaret are, and casts them in a sympathetic light as two rather lonely people, who have seen life pass by all too quickly and can't help but wonder what might have been. "That's one of my favorite episodes," said David Renwick. "I felt they played it so wonderfully, and they got the whole feel and chemistry of their relationship, particularly when she got to the moment when she's talking about the baby they had lost. It was just so poignant. It was just a half an hour of real time and I felt it was very real. Obviously there were some quite stylized comic moments . . . but it was nice to set that challenge up." Susan Belbin added, ". . . To hold an audience's attention for thirty minutes of real time in the bedroom was the first risk we took. But by that time the audience knew the characters sufficiently [for us] to be able to play half of that in the dark as well!"

The series later presents an even more daring episode: a solo performance by Richard Wilson for the entire half hour. Belbin had asked Renwick several months earlier to consider writing a solo episode. The episode entitled "The Trial" has Victor stuck at home waiting for a phone call about his impending jury duty requirements. Margaret is away for the day so he's left to his own devices to entertain himself for the afternoon. As he wanders through the house, he allows the most inconsequential matters to command his attention. Of course, a day with Victor wouldn't be complete without several angry phone calls to incompetent shop managers, and this day is no different. The simple task of preparing a snack of baked beans on toast comes to a grinding halt when, to his utter disbelief, he extracts a man's toupee out of the bread loaf. The episode ends with a slow pull-back shot of his house as the air fills with his telephone tirade to the bakery.

A clever production technique developed by Susan Belbin for the studio tapings (and most noticeable in the solo episode) enabled the set of the Meldrews' home to be truly three-dimensional. Instead of seeing the action from the same few angles through the "fourth wall," we're able to follow the actors all throughout the house. This was accomplished by inserting removable walls wherever necessary, depending on where the cameras had to shoot, even if it meant blocking the studio audience's view for a scene (studio monitors helped keep the action visible). As Belbin explained, "I wanted to bring as much realism into the show, given that it was still a situation comedy. I myself was tiring slightly of the three walls and people came in one door and sat down and talked to one another. Husbands and wives don't sit down and talk to one another—somebody's doing the washing up, somebody's reading the paper in the living room, and they shout through to one another. I wanted to create that truthfulness."

Perhaps the most innovative episode of all, called "The Beast in the Cage," takes place entirely in Victor's car, as the Meldrews sit trapped in the middle of an insufferable traffic jam. They are unable to move ahead more than twenty feet at a time. The episode was shot on location on a Vauxhall test track, where the simulated jam was painstakingly arranged. It took eight days to shoot. Here we're treated to a choice example of how Victor's patience and tolerance of others can be so easily pushed to the limit. Early on, it appears that he and Margaret are to share another episode with only each other to talk to for the duration. But about ten minutes into the episode, their friend Mrs. Warboys suddenly appears from out of nowhere and gets into the back seat! We then learn that she had been with the Meldrews all along, but since the traffic wasn't really moving anywhere, she had decided to take a restroom break across the road. This is a fine example of how writer Renwick often leaves out bits of information that the characters know but the audience doesn't, until it's necessary. This particular gag works to great effect and is Renwick's way of trying to vary the sitcom structure. "The trouble is that situation comedy can become so formulaic if you're not careful," he said. "I do like, where possible, to bring changes on the formula, so it isn't always the same old . . . like the feed-line/repost or smart

One Foot in the Grave is currently slated to return to production—with the original cast—early in 2000.

reply. It's very prevalent in American comedy, which is not always to my taste."

As the afternoon in traffic wears on, Victor naturally finds cause to bicker with drivers on all sides of him. One such antagonist gets a call on his car phone. Oddly enough, the call is for Victor. The caller is the driver directly behind him, who wants him to move up further (even though there are only a few feet to spare), thus giving Victor additional cause to vent.

Susan Belbin's philosophy is that the TV viewing audience deserves a sitcom that makes them laugh as well as think, just as a drama would. "With *One Foot in the Grave* you have to watch the full thirty minutes, otherwise a lot of it won't make sense. And the viewing public caught on to that, and they now know when they sit down to watch it that they can't take their eyes off it."

As seen in "Who Will Buy?," a rather striking feature of *One Foot in the Grave* is its tendency to include the frequent plot twist that is actually quite sad, even tragic. For the unsuspecting viewer, the sudden shift of emotional gears could be unnerving. One episode features Victor and a stonemason he has hired to fix a brick wall in the backyard. Before long, Victor's complaints get the better of him, culminating with a shot of him buried up to his neck in the garden soil. It's a hilarious moment, but it's suddenly tempered by Margaret's appearance in the garden to break the news that her mother has died. "The predicaments and misfortunes are unbearable and tragic a lot of the time, because that's life, it's real," said David Renwick. "Most of the surprises are comic surprises. But now and again they might be tragic surprises. If you just come to the tragedy and there is a moment of jollity afterwards, it's a wonderful release. More often than not I try to finish an episode on an up note. I never really believe that anything I write is there to give people a harrowing time! Ultimately there's a feel-good factor about it." And *One Foot in the Grave* provides it in abundance, with a comic inventiveness that has earned the series such widespread respect.

THE PIGLET FILES

LWT
1990-1991
14 Episodes

Written by Paul Minett and Brian Leveson
Produced by Robin Carr

Cast:

PETER CHAPMAN ("PIGLET") . . . Nicholas Lyndhurst
MAJOR MAURICE DRUMMOND . . . Clive Francis
ANDREW MAXWELL . . . . John Ringham
DEXTER . . . . Michael Percival
LEWIS . . . . Steven Law
FLINT . . . . Louise Catt
SARAH . . . . Serena Evans

This contemporary spoof of British Intelligence spydom may be vaguely reminiscent of the American *Get Smart* series of the 1960s. However, here we have not one bumbling Maxwell Smart type, but a whole team of them.

Nicholas Lyndhurst plays computer electronics whiz and college professor Peter Chapman, who has been targeted by MI-5 (the British CIA) for recruitment. In order to make him available to accept the new position when offered, the agency arranges to have him fired from his teaching job and then referred to a "recruitment agency." He meets his future boss, Maurice Drummond, and Drummond's boss, Andrew Maxwell, who explain that Peter will be developing high-tech spying devices and teaching others to use them. Without being given much choice, Peter signs the Official Secrets Act, forbidding him to tell anyone, even his wife, of his new role in the agency. It's pretty heady stuff, and he tries to comfort himself by asking Drummond, "I'm not likely to be shot by an enemy agent or anything?" To which Drummond assures him, "Good Lord, no. You're far more likely to get shot by one of ours." The only aspect of the job that truly impresses Peter is the traditional assignment of a code name for each operative. However, he finds that the next name on the list is "Piglet." As a rather pointed joke, Drummond henceforth addresses him as Piglet at all times (even though none of the others on the team have ever used their own code names).

Piglet's cohorts make his new job more nerve-wracking than any enemy spy could ever hope to do. Like the father of unruly offspring, he tends to spend most of his time rescuing the others from near-disasters, which in their business can lead to international crises. Dexter, for example, is a moron and perpetual thorn in Drummond's side. He is prone to mishaps such as squirting ketchup on surveillance camera lenses. His partner, Lewis, tends to shake his head at Dexter's incompetence only to plunge headfirst into trouble himself. Thankfully, Flint, the female (and most rational) member of the group, demonstrates quick thinking as well as some unexpected muscle when needed.

In "Now You See It" we learn that the French have developed the "Black Ghost" device, which renders aircraft invisible to radar. The team has been saddled with an American CIA agent, MacLaine, who behaves as a one-man commando unit. His strong-arm tactics enrage Drummond, who sends him out of the briefing room so the team can learn of a new development.

A French fighter jet has crashed into the sea near a British naval ship. Drummond explains that the Black Ghost box was onboard the plane, and probably caused the malfunction. The British have recovered it and plan to have it analyzed and replaced before the French can arrive at the scene. Piglet is assigned to inspect the device, and the others are to accompany him. Arriving at the lab, they discover that MacLaine, having overheard Drummond's briefing, has beaten them to it. He has tied up the professor who was to work with Piglet, and takes the Black Ghost at gunpoint. He locks the others in a back room. When the men can't figure a way to get out, the exasperated Flint mutters "Men!" before kicking the door clear off its hinges. They later find that MacLaine has been mugged, and the Black Ghost stolen. When it's learned that Swedish spies, of all people, are the culprits, Piglet wonders, "What are they gonna do, make it an optional extra on a Volvo?"

An attempt to intercept the Swedes' getaway by private plane results in Piglet at the controls of the plane, flying out of control and buzzing around the airfield. Lewis begins an attempt to talk Piglet down, but when asked what to do next, he concedes, "I don't know. In the movies they usually send for Charlton Heston." Piglet quite unintentionally lands in France, and is flown back to England. At MI-5, he informs an angry Drummond that the infamous box wasn't the Black Ghost after all, but rather a thermostat mistakenly removed by Navy divers. However, Piglet redeems himself by explaining that he secretly removed the real Black Ghost from the French military plane that flew him back to England. As is the case in many of the series' episodes, Piglet and his colleagues have somehow succeeded despite themselves.

While Nicholas Lyndhurst later continued his string of sitcom successes with *Goodnight Sweetheart*, co-star Serena Evans found herself in a more substantial role opposite Rowan Atkinson in *The Thin Blue Line*.

WAITING FOR GOD

BBC
1990–1994
45 episodes, 2 specials

Written by Michael Aitkens
Produced and directed by Gareth Gwenlan

Available on home video in the U.S.

Cast:

DIANA TRENT . . . . Stephanie Cole
TOM BALLARD . . . . Graham Crowden
HARVEY BANES . . . . Daniel Hill
JANE . . . . Jane Duvitski
GEOFFREY . . . . Andrew Tourell
MARION . . . . Sandra Payne

Harvey "The Idiot" Banes (Daniel Hill, left, with Jane Duvitski), about to throw another monkey wrench into Tom and Diana's peaceful retirement. Chances are he'll be sorry. *BBC Worldwide*

A retirement home might not seem a likely setting for a comedy series at first glance. The residents are old, often ill, and seem to indeed be waiting for God. And yet this program is a genuinely funny, thoughtful, and even inspiring comedy brought to life by stars Graham Crowden and Stephanie Cole.

Creator/writer Michael Aitkens recalls the initial inspiration for *Waiting for God*: "I was living in Australia about twelve years ago, and they opened a place not far from me called the Bayview Retirement Village. And I thought, 'Ah, there's a good arena.' Because when you write these sort of things you're always looking for a new arena. Basically characters and jokes are much the same, but the setting is the thing you're looking for. And I suggested doing it in Australia, but I found I couldn't cast it well enough." He sat on it for a few years, returned to England and offered it to the

BBC. An executive who considered putting the show on Sunday evening worried about the title and how viewers would likely confuse it for a religious program. But Aitkens couldn't think of a better title. The executive let the title stay but moved the show to Thursdays.

As the series opens, we meet Tom Ballard, a retired accountant and widower who has been living with his son and daughter-in-law, Geoffrey and Marion. Tom has decided it's time to move on, although the only place he can really move to is the beautiful Bayview Retirement Home. Geoffrey, dull but good-hearted, has mixed feelings about Tom moving out, but the nasty, drunken Marion is glad to see Tom go. The feeling is mutual.

Upon his arrival, Tom meets Harvey Banes, the soft-spoken but rather mean-spirited manager of Bayview. Harvey's homely, Bible-quoting assistant Jane worships the ground he walks on for reasons known only to her, but he doesn't want her to touch him, even by accident. Harvey's only real concern is maintaining a budget acceptable to Bayview's board of directors. He's also used to overseeing submissive residents who don't cause trouble, but before long he realizes that Tom Ballard is hardly the shy, retiring type, so to speak. Tom enjoys battling boredom and confounding others by slipping into sudden imitations of emus and other wildlife, as well as claiming to be various other identities, both famous and otherwise. He often sits in an open-eyed trance until he's ready to explain, with a perfectly straight face, that he had just completed his climb up Mount Everest with Edmund Hillary. Other flights of fancy take him to all corners of the Earth with a dazzling assortment of shapely movie stars from Hollywood's golden age. And he'll happily greet a doctor with the exclamation, "What ho, quack!"

Tom finds himself living next door to Diana Trent, a frustrated and bitter spinster unamused by his fanciful and imaginative diversions. Unlike Tom, Diana has lived a life full of adventure as a photojournalist. She never married but enjoyed countless affairs and worldwide travel. Her exciting career came to an end when age and failing health gave her little choice but to pack it in. She tries to hide her loneliness behind a relentlessly cynical and sometimes cruel persona, but no amount of cynicism can dampen her reluctant amusement and fascination with Tom's joie de vivre. She even seems rather envious of his ability to enjoy who and where he is. They soon become unlikely allies in a joint venture to improve the quality of life at Bayview (which involves battling Harvey "The Idiot" Banes at every turn), and to make the most of life in the time they have left.

Tom and Diana's feisty nature, which they employ constructively in their fight to maintain their dignity, often must give way to the inevitabilities of their age. Their first crisis occurs in the second series, when Diana falls and breaks her hip. She makes for a miserable hospital patient, but she confides to Tom that fear is the major force now driving her. Not only might her hip replacement operation cause her to miss her niece's upcoming wedding, but she sees her impending need of a steel-frame walker as the true and unwelcome arrival of old age. "My first false bit," she sighs

about her new hip. "It'll be my teeth next. Then the heart, lungs—stick around long enough and you become somebody else." But despite the physical and psychological setbacks, she arrives at the wedding more or less on time, and accompanied by a group of her peers all using walkers like her own.

The fourth series brought a big change for Tom and Diana. Upon learning that her invested money has disappeared into a black hole of a company's bankruptcy, Diana is shaken by her uncertain future. Tom in the meantime informs Harvey that his room is intolerably damp, and demands new accommodations. But Tom is not to move into his new suite alone. A reluctant Diana, with nowhere else to go, is to be his official flatmate. Predictably enough, the sparks fly. Their new flat is apparently not big enough for the both of them. Diana soon flees the situation to take on nanny work for her niece's baby. Tom is glad to be rid of her at first, but her unwelcome replacement is Geoffrey, Tom's tragically boring son who has finally left his wife. Eventually, Diana tires of being a nanny and returns in time to save Tom from dying of boredom.

One of the most poignant of the subsequent episodes concerns Tom and the sudden onset of a prostate problem. It manifests itself one night in a most embarrassing way, and even he can't summon his sense of humor to hide his humiliation and fear from Diana. But after a short hospital stay and a bit of tough love from Diana, Tom gets himself back into fighting form.

Eventually, Tom pops the question to Diana. Her response is less than heartwarming. She has resisted marriage all her life, and especially doesn't relish marrying into a dysfunctional family like Tom's, but he won't give up. To prove his virility, he embarks on driving lessons, only to crash into the driving school's plate glass window on the first day. Later, in another attempt at emotional blackmail, Tom parachutes onto the grounds of Bayview only to get caught up in a tree. Despite his life-threatening stunt, Diana rejects his proposal yet again. Unswayed, he takes to bungee jumping, but is spared his first jump when she finally gives in and agrees to marry him. However, her long list of ground rules are not those of a blushing bride. Meanwhile, Harvey's proposal to Jane, for reasons no loftier than to improve his upwardly mobile

Reluctant soulmates Diana (Stephanie Cole) and Tom (Graham Crowden). *BBC Worldwide*

Despite the occasional medical and/or psychological crises among the patients of Bayview, *Waiting for God* shines in its laugh-out-loud humor and in-depth characterizations. "I was working as sort of a propaganda arm of Age Concern," said Michael Aitkens, "which is an old people's organization here that looks after them. I'm trying to put in subliminally some preaching about various things like how to deal with prostate problems, hip replacements, that sort of thing. It never worried me about getting humor out of it—it's the first time I've thought about it, really."

The show won the Writer's Guild Comedy Award in 1992, the same year Stephanie Cole won for Best Comedy Actress. It was well-deserved recognition for a program that treats the elderly with dignity and defers to their experience and wisdom.

Old people are like public libraries, Michael Aitkens said. "They know an awful lot, and all you have to do is listen to them and you can take quantum leaps forward without having to suffer it yourself. But nobody ever learns that lesson."

Aitkens began each script with one or two ideas, usually one idea for the plot and another for what he's trying to say about the elderly in that episode. One episode that caused a bit of publicity had Tom and Diana finally winding up in bed together. Rarely had a television series acknowledged that people in their seventies could still enjoy sex.

Series producer Gareth Gwenlan feels a show with elderly lead characters can be appealing to viewers of all ages. "Obviously the older people related to it directly, middle-aged parents could see the problems coming up when they have to look after their elderly relatives, and the younger people conventionally enjoy their grandparents. The more outrageous they are, the more they like them. There's often a great bond between the teenager and the older person."

social status, has caused Jane's blushes to balance Diana's prenuptial scowl.

The wedding day arrives to find Jane shell-shocked and hung over from the girls' previous night out at a Chippendale's club. A schedule mix-up has caused the wedding and a funeral procession to coincide in the chapel. Once the pallbearers are shooed away, Harvey and Jane finally tie the knot. Their first kiss draws gasps from the guests, as a newly enlightened Jane practically devours the unsuspecting Harvey. Finally it's Tom and Diana's turn. When they're asked to take their vows, Tom surprises everyone by refusing to take Diana as his wife. He knows she is still against the marriage, and is only at the altar to please him. Likewise, his love for her and respect for her true feelings have prompted him to save her any further discomfort. Their commitment to each other has indeed transcended the conventions of ritual wedding vows.

> Stephanie Cole, so convincing as a crotchety woman in her seventies, was barely into her fifties when she began her role as Diana.

KEEPING UP APPEARANCES

BBC
1990-1994
5 Series, 40 Episodes,
4 Christmas Specials

Written by Roy Clarke
Produced and directed by Harold Snoad

Available on home video in the U.S.

Cast:

HYACINTH BUCKET . . . . Patricia Routledge
RICHARD BUCKET . . . . Clive Swift
DAISY . . . . Judy Cornwell
ROSE . . . . Shirley Stelfox (series 1)
. . . . Mary Millar (series 2-5)
ONSLOW . . . . Geoffrey Hughes
LIZ . . . . Josephine Tewson
EMMET . . . . David Griffin
MAJOR . . . . Peter Cellier

Hyacinth (Patricia Routledge)
simply will not have Richard
(Clive Swift) be seen in public
with lint on his suit.
BBC Worldwide

What is it about Hyacinth Bucket (pronounced "Bouquet," as she will note tirelessly) that sends even the most casual of acquaintances scurrying out of sight when they see her approaching? The answer lies at the heart of her offbeat appeal in *Keeping up Appearances*. Hyacinth is an aristocratic wannabe trapped in the body of a stout, sixtyish suburban housewife. Her raison d'être is to devise whatever strategy is necessary to cross paths with Britain's upper class, win their good graces, and wedge herself into a new niche, however ill-fitting it may be.

It is the sheer force of Hyacinth's personality that makes those around her cringe when contact is imminent. She can be polite on the surface, trilling on in her singsong voice, but soon reveals herself to be hopelessly snobbish, overbearing, and demanding. She refuses to take no for an answer when inviting friends for tea or to her infamous candle-

light suppers. Nor is she above accepting invitations to desirable social events when none are actually offered. She is also a control freak who rarely maintains control of her circumstances for very long.

It comes as no surprise that Hyacinth's husband Richard must endure life as the most henpecked husband in the hemisphere. Quiet, practical, and possessing the patience of a saint, Richard is resigned to the fact that his rather meek nature is no match for his dynamo of a wife. He also knows there's no use in trying to dissuade her schemes to enhance her social standing, so he quietly goes along (usually as her chauffeur) and does what he can to avoid disaster.

Hyacinth's climb up the social ladder is often sabotaged, in her mind anyway, by her own family, whom she sees as a constant source of embarrassment. Truth be told, she has some cause for feeling that way. Her frumpy sister Daisy is married to a beer-guzzling, unshaven couch potato named Onslow who rarely dresses beyond his undershirt. Onslow is a mild-mannered bloke, but his easygoing nature is almost sloth-like and his sense of romance dissipated long ago. Daisy refuses to give up hope that she can rekindle the fire. Hyacinth's other sister Rose lives with Daisy and Onslow in their sloppy home. Rose not only dresses years younger than her age in her quest to land a man, but her sense of fashion can most kindly be described as provocative. Her gaudy outfits brazenly show off her long, slender legs as well as other accoutrements. The sisters' father also has a knack for causing trouble. Daddy has lost most of his marbles long ago, and now keeps himself entertained by lurking about the neighborhood dressed in army fatigues and harassing young ladies as they pass by.

Hyacinth's next-door neighbors must bear the brunt of her ways on a daily basis. Liz, whose husband is forever working in Saudi Arabia, offers little resistance to Hyacinth's invitations to tea and candlelight suppers. Once inside the Bucket residence however, Liz becomes a bundle of nerves. The harder she tries to keep her teacup and saucer steady, the clumsier she gets. Her recently divorced brother Emmet has moved in with her. He's a music teacher who goes to great pains to avoid Hyacinth's impromptu singing auditions.

The finest moments of *Keeping up Appearances* occur just as Hyacinth is about to score a few points with whomever she is trying to impress, only to catch sight of her motley relatives arriving to join the occasion. Sometimes the distant sound of Onslow's car backfiring is enough warning that Hyacinth's best laid plans are about to fall apart.

One episode opens with Hyacinth on the phone to a furniture store. She's making plans for the delivery of her three-piece suite, "an exact replica of the one at Sandringham Palace." She insists that the delivery van display the royal warrant decal on both sides, so she can impress the "pseudo-hyphenated" snobs across the street, the Barker-Finches. She prepares for the delivery by directing Richard to place traffic cones on the street in front of the house, along with the sign "No Parking—Delivery Imminent." She then calls Daisy to offer her the old furniture set.

Later, Hyacinth has Richard stall the van driver until she can call the Barker-Finches to draw

The family may be Hyacinth's, but the decor is strictly Daisy and Onslow's. Joining Richard and Hyacinth are Onslow (Geoffrey Hughes), Daisy (Judy Cornwell), and Rose (Mary Millar).
BBC Worldwide

their attention to the delivery. But as the driver goes around the corner to kill time, the van gets into an accident. Onslow, Daisy, and Rose then arrive in their dilapidated truck—hardly the sight Hyacinth wants her neighbors to see. "You know I love my family," she tells Richard, "but that's no reason to have to acknowledge them in broad daylight." Out of desperation, she pretends to give Onslow directions just to get them out of sight. Before long Onlsow's truck returns, with the moving men and new furniture all squeezed onto the back. So much for Hyacinth's latest attempt to impress the neighbors.

Another episode opens with Hyacinth backseat driving as she and Richard head to Chesford Grange Golf Club for a weekend. They've been invited by their acquaintance, the Major, and his wife. "It means we're upwardly mobile, dear," smirks Hyacinth. Once at the club's hotel, she puts the staff through the mill with her snooty demands and conducts a white glove inspection of the room.

All appears satisfactory, except for the noise from room 210 next door, where a libidinous couple is enjoying a noisy romp. The Major, who is actually scheming to act upon his long held desires for Hyacinth, has arrived at the hotel without his wife. He also feigns a bad leg and arranges for Richard to play golf with another partner.

In the garden, Hyacinth must interrupt her friendly pestering of her fellow hotel guests when she spots Onslow's car coming up the drive. Of course, her first instinct is to hide, but she soon runs into Rose stepping out of the notorious room 210. Onslow and Daisy are there to pick up Rose. To avoid further embarrassment, Hyacinth accepts the Major's invitation for a country drive in his roadster convertible. But once they come upon a secluded spot, the Major turns into a groping octopus. Hyacinth struggles with him (and her seatbelt) before fleeing over a fence and across a field populated with sheep. Back at the hotel, Onslow and Daisy spot her coming up the road, her mud-splattered dress in tatters. She flashes a half-hearted smile to the other curious guests, and informs Richard that it's time to go home.

As in this episode, many *Keeping up Appearances* episodes contain a good deal of slapstick, usually involving Hyacinth in some physical entanglement at a critical moment. The slapstick is that much funnier when juxtaposed with Hyacinth's obsession with maintaining her composure and coiffure at all times, especially in public. "Apart from being a splendid actress, [Patricia Routledge] is a wonderful physical clown," said writer Roy Clarke. "And I never realized that until I saw her in action, and when you realize what she

can do physically, then you think, yes, you've got to exploit that."

Producer Harold Snoad worked with Patricia Routledge on a good bit of the physical gags that were not supplied by Roy Clarke. "I don't think Roy actually ever wrote any visuals at first," said Snoad. "When I started to work with Pat, I realized that she was a very good farceur, and it was me who used to give her bits of business which weren't in the script but embellished what was there. And she did that extremely well. And [Josephine Tewson] who plays Liz next door is a very good farceur. And I think Roy noticed this and put in a little bit of this and a little bit of that. But on the whole, it was just that I got together with Pat in rehearsals and it became a well-known sort of trademark."

Patricia Routledge won the Top TV Comedy Actress award at the 1991 Writers' Guild Comedy Awards, and was also named the 1992 BBC Personality of the Year by the Variety Club of Great Britain. In 1997, she took on a new character, Hetty Wainthropp, a bored housewife who embarks on a new career as a private detective, in the four-part drama series *Hetty Wainthropp Investigates*. It was seen as part of PBS's long-running *Mystery!* series. In July of 1998, Routledge was the subject of an installment of the BBC documentary series *Funny Women*. Television critics, in reviewing the episode, took the opportunity to once again praise her comedic talents.

Actor Geoffrey Hughes (Onslow) provided the "voice" of Paul McCartney in the Beatles' 1968 animated classic *Yellow Submarine*.

THE BRITTAS EMPIRE

BBC
1991-1996
7 Series, 51 Episodes, 1 Special

*Written by Richard Fegen and
Andrew Norriss
Produced and directed by Mike Stephens*

Cast:

GORDON BRITTAS	Chris Barrie
LAURA	Julia St. John
COLIN	Michael Burns
HELEN	Pippa Heywood
CAROL	Harriet Thorpe
JULIE	Judy Flynn
GAVIN	Tim Marriott
TIM	Russel Porter
LINDA	Jill Greenacre

Waiting for the other shoe—or piece of the building—to drop are (*clockwise from top*): Colin (Michael Burns), Julie (Judy Flynn), Laura (Julia St. John), Gordon (Chris Barrie), Tim (Russel Porter), and Gavin (Tim Marriott). *BBC Worldwide*

The Brittas Empire has been hailed as "the *Fawlty Towers* of the 1990s," and deservedly so. While it has not enjoyed the recognition of John Cleese's landmark sitcom, this fast-paced, outrageous series full of inventive gags shares much of the same style. In both cases, the cast of characters (especially the leads) manage to turn molehills of problems into mountains of catastrophe.

We first meet Gordon Brittas as he assumes the role of manager at Whitbury New Town Leisure Centre, a fitness and health club. An eternal optimist, he prefers to downplay the fact that his previous tenure as a leisure center manager in Aldershot ended with him being more or less run out of town. Instead, he's ready to make a fresh start. As he introduces himself to the staff and establishes his philosophy of life and leisure cen-

ters, they quickly size up their new boss. Gordon is well meaning enough. He has a dream, one in which world harmony is achieved through sport and friendly competition, and he intends to pursue his dream for the rest of his life. The only drawback to his pursuit is his peculiar knack of driving those around him absolutely crazy. Of course, he is totally oblivious to the effect he has on people. He is an incessant stickler for proper procedure (no matter how trivial), insists on employing a hands-on approach (no matter how incapable he is for the task), and somehow manages to treat his staff and customers in a manner that might be best described as cheerfully condescending. Whenever he takes it upon himself to "help out" at the front reception desk, Gordon inevitably transforms a handful of docile customers into an angry mob. Thanks to a rollicking performance by Chris Barrie (Arnold Rimmer on *Red Dwarf*), Gordon Brittas in action is truly a sight to behold.

Despite Gordon's uncanny talent for courting disaster singlehandedly, his constant striving to maintain an efficient leisure center is often undermined by his own eccentric staff. Receptionist Carol Parkinson rarely gets through the day without sobbing from the emotional upheavals of postpartum depression, even though she keeps her baby Ben tucked away in a nearby cupboard drawer next to her reception desk. One of the deputy managers, Colin Weatherby, is a fiercely loyal and industrious employee if not a very hygienic one. He is perpetually nursing a variety of skin infections, injuries, and any number of ailments involving repugnant bodily secretions. His accident-prone ways have prompted Gordon to dub him "a dead pigeon in the jet turbines of management." Staffers Gavin and Tim are a gay couple, unknown to the highly moral Brittas of course, but casually accepted by the rest of the staff. Gordon's secretary Julie assists her boss when the mood strikes her, and not a minute sooner.

Then there's Gordon's wife, Helen. By her own admission, she found Gordon quite charming when they first met. But a few years of marriage has turned her into a walking nervous breakdown, addicted to Valium and perpetually carrying on affairs right under Gordon's nose. She knows her husband better than anyone, so whenever she stops by the center for a visit, she's rarely fazed to find the place knee-deep in crisis.

Only Laura Lancing, the center's assistant manager, represents the voice of reason when all around her is crumbling to the ground (sometimes literally). She is attractive, logical, and the one person the others can turn to in their more dire moments under Gordon's command. On rare occasion, Laura even attempts a heart-to-heart talk with her boss, with the glimmer of hope that he might recognize how his maddening ways tend to invite disaster and nudge his staff to near-mutiny. Julia St. John as Laura shines as the eye of the storm over *The Brittas Empire*, but even Laura often finds herself helplessly swept up in the chaos.

Richard Fegen and Andrew Norriss originally conceived their new series to take place in a community center (a public meeting hall for various organizations and their events). When they realized another series used the same setting, they decided

Gordon Brittas (Chris Barrie) and his loyal deputies, Colin (Michael Burns) and Laura (Julia St. John). *BBC Worldwide*

on a leisure center. A real leisure center in Hampshire was used for the location scenes, such as exterior shots and those at the indoor pool. The choice proved to be an excellent one. The flexibility of the setting, like that of *Fawlty Towers*, allows for any number of things to happen. "It had the advantage that the public keeps coming in," said co-creator/co-writer Andrew Norriss, "though we had one of our rules which was that the public always had to be sane and decent ordinary people, and if anything weird happened it had to come from Brittas. He was the only one who was allowed to do anything strange, except Colin was allowed to be strange as well."

As Julia St. John recalled, "I read the first script and thought that it was extremely well-written and very subtle, as well as all of the more overt anarchy. There were some lovely subtle things, which I think is the hallmark of it, actually. And each episode has three or four storylines, which all get resolved at the end. . . . It was a hoot. For the five series that I did, it was tremendous fun."

In "Generations," Brittas encounters a farmer fixing his disabled van in the parking lot, with his prize-winning (and pregnant) cow in tow. Gordon orders them off the property, but becomes distracted with other matters, such as Carol's latest pregnancy (in its ninth month). The cow wanders into the building and eventually onto a squash court. As fate would have it, both Carol and the cow have inadvertently eaten Colin's exotic leaves used for, among other things, helping induce labor. They both go into labor shortly thereafter. The concerned farmer encounters a gynecologist who is just finishing a game on the next squash court, and offers him a hefty sum to deliver the calf. Meanwhile, the local vet arrives. Gordon can't wait for the ambulance so he sends the vet to deliver Carol's baby in the sauna. "Would it help if we got her on all fours?" he asks the vet in all seriousness, "If she's the other way around, it might help you get your bearings." Back on the squash court, the gynecologist prepares to deliver the calf with the help of his portable equipment, monitors, and soothing classical music. Somehow, both mothers and their newborns (Carol has twins) get through it unscathed.

A later episode opens with Laura about to go on an interview for a manager's position at a leisure center in London. Upon hearing the news, Helen arrives in a state of panic. She pleads with Gordon to somehow stop Laura, her best friend and only glimmer of sanity at the center. "She's all this place has got, Gordon!" Helen pleads, "Can't you doctor her references or something?"

In the time it takes for Laura to go on her interview and return, all hell breaks loose at the center yet again. Colin, stumbling about in a daze from a minor head injury, is sent to turn up the heat in the pool for a baptism ceremony that afternoon. In trying to save his deputy from hurting himself, Gordon succeeds only in accidentally dropping a heating unit into the pool during the ceremony, electrocuting the participants. In the meantime, an irate customer from the rifle range goes to war with a defective coffee machine and a frazzled Gordon fires Carol for keeping her babies and their toys in her desk drawers. Laura returns in time to witness the baptism "victims" spread across the reception area floor and the coffee machine warrior shooting his rifle into the air, demanding his cup of coffee. Of course, she helps restore order with minimum effort, and has even turned down the offer for the London job, much to Helen's delight and Gordon's bewilderment.

The writers knew by the end of series 2 that they needed to give Gordon Brittas a tad more depth, to avoid making him too much of a cartoon. "Because he's so horrid and awful," said Andrew Norriss, "it was important, we eventually found, not to just laugh at him but to find a human side to it and a warmth somewhere. And Laura provides that probably more than any of the others."

By the third series, the show was at full throttle. It became a happy marriage of good writers and a cast with good characters. To make things even more interesting, the later episodes reveal Laura's unexpected attraction to Brittas. Gordon seems oblivious to this, but he nonetheless has come to realize Laura's value as a friend. "She was able to see the better side of his character," explained Julia St. John, "and indeed he did endear himself to her." But true romance was never in the cards, due to Gordon's high moral standards. "I think he wouldn't have permitted himself to go the full length with her," added St. John, "and that's what saves him. And also by the fifth series Laura's husband is back, the American billionaire . . . but it's interesting that Laura and Brittas are very drawn to each other."

One particular moment that perfectly defines both Laura's affection for Gordon as well as the program's black humor comes at the end of an episode in which a mysterious figure in black makes several assassination attempts on Brittas. The culprit turns out to be a member of the parish choir, whose numbers have dwindled to virtually nothing since Gordon joined. Of course, his attempts on Gordon's life find all the wrong targets. However, Gordon does end up in the hospital's intensive care unit, after being hit by a truck while crossing the road on his way home (his insistence of having the right of way was no match for the oncoming truck). As Helen sits beside her unconscious husband, Laura joins her. Helen wonders out loud whether it might be easier on everyone else if Gordon simply didn't recover. Laura is startled by the suggestion at first, then confesses she would miss him, despite his annoying tendencies.

"But what I always end up remembering," she adds, "is that there's never any malice. He doesn't hate anybody. He cares about the center and all the people in it. He wants more than anything to help. He really does have a dream. And even though things never quite work out the way he wanted, the fact that he tries, that he keeps on trying—well, I think that's worth something." Helen thinks it over, agrees with Laura, and reaches over to plug the life support machines back into the wall socket!

Andrew Norriss considers any comparison between *The Brittas Empire* and *Fawlty Towers* (and there are several valid ones) to be a great compliment. The writers of both series devoted much more time to writing each episode—about a month—than is common in British television.

They saw virtually no boundaries in the story possibilities, including blowing up the leisure center at the end of the fourth series. Norriss recalled, "Blowing it up was quite fun, so I think we've blown it up once in most of the series . . . We thought [the series] might come back but we didn't know, and it seemed a nice sort of end."

There was life in *The Brittas Empire* yet, but the end of series 5 seemed the end for sure. "The one we really thought was the end was one where we killed him," Norriss said. The story has Gordon rescuing Carol as the leisure center, in one of its many calamities, collapses around them. Carol survives, but Gordon doesn't. We then see Gordon at the Pearly Gates, getting on Saint Peter's nerves after he's allowed in. "I'm terribly proud of that one," said Norriss. "The last quarter of an hour, the cast acting and the rest of it, and the story, it's wonderful."

Surely this incident would mark the end of Gordon Brittas. The attendees at his funeral are convinced of it—until they hear a faint knocking from inside his coffin. . . .

AS TIME GOES BY

BBC
1992–
8 Series, 54 Episodes

Written by Bob Larbey
Produced by Sydney Lotterby

Available on home video in the U.S.

Cast:

LIONEL HARDCASTLE . . . . Geoffrey Palmer
JEAN PARGETTER . . . . Judi Dench
JUDY . . . . Moira Booker
ALISTAIR DEACON . . . . Philip Bretherton
SANDY . . . . Jenny Funnell

Seated (*left to right*): Lionel (Geoffrey Palmer), Jean (Judi Dench), and Sandy (Jenny Funnell). Standing are Alistair (Philip Bretherton) and Judith (Moira Booker). *BBC Worldwide*

The intriguing scenario of *As Time Goes By* was conceived by veteran comedy writer Colin Bostock-Smith. Bob Larbey took up the scriptwriting duties. (Larbey and his former writing partner John Esmonde created *The Good Life, Ever Decreasing Circles*, and other Britcoms. Esmonde later moved to Spain to pursue a career as a novelist.)

As the opening episode unfolds, we learn that Lionel and Jean were young sweethearts in the early 1950s when Lionel was sent off to the Korean War. Once in Korea, Lionel wrote to Jean, just as she had written to him. Somehow though, their letters never reached each other, and each concluded that the other had decided to abandon the relationship. Thirty years later, the widowed Jean is owner of a successful secretarial agency. Lionel, having been a coffee plantation owner in Kenya for most of the intervening years, has been persuaded to write a book about his life. His need of a secretary leads

him by chance to Jean's agency. Once there, Lionel meets Jean's daughter and office assistant, Judy. Lionel takes an interest in Judy and invites her out to dinner. Through a series of chance remarks over the next few days and with a few probing questions for Judy, both Lionel and Jean independently discover that their paths are indeed about to cross again. Judy sets up their initial meeting, which is awkward, poignant, and funny. Once they discover how their letters never reached each other, they can't help but think of what might have been. The big question becomes what to do now. Try to rekindle an old flame, or go their separate ways again?

Lionel and Jean cautiously resume casual dating, much to the delight of Judy and of Lionel's agent, Alistair. As the series progresses, the love affair blooms. The natural course of events leads them to decide to move in together under the same roof. But who's roof will it be? After a few misun-

Alistair's enthusiasm doesn't always rub off on Lionel and Jean. *BBC Worldwide*

A new set of episodes of *As Time Goes By*—with the original cast—will be taped in early 2000.

derstandings and an uncomfortable stalemate, Lionel finally volunteers to give up his modest apartment. But moving in with Jean and Judy brings about a new set of compromises to be worked out. In the meantime, Alistair has found an American TV company interested in making Lionel and Jean's romantic story into a mini-series. Lionel finds himself on the spot to come up with a suitable treatment to pitch to the TV executives in Los Angeles.

To complicate life further, Jean's assistant Sandy temporarily moves into the Pargetter house as well. Lionel, having been divorced for years and preferring to think of himself as rather set in his ways, now finds himself sharing a house with three women.

Lionel and Jean eventually marry (in series 4), but the story doesn't end there, as the notorious American miniseries of their life nears completion and broadcast.

The familiar faces and obvious professional chemistry between Geoffrey Palmer and Judi Dench make *As Time Goes By* an easygoing pleasure. Palmer is by now an icon of sorts in the Britcom world. Judi Dench (who is actually Dame Judi Dench, since receiving the OBE in 1988) has won six BAFTA Awards. In addition to her Academy Award nomination for her role as Queen Victoria in *Mrs. Brown*, Dench won the 1999 Oscar for Best Supporting Actress for her portrayal of Queen Elizabeth in *Shakespeare in Love*.

SIDE BY SIDE

BBC
1992-1993
13 Episodes

Written by Richard Ommanney
Produced by Nic Phillips

Cast:

GILLY BELL	Louisa Rix
VINCE TULLEY	Gareth Hunt
STELLA TULLEY	Julia Deakin
KATIE BELL	Mia Fothergill
TERRY SHANE	Alex Walkenshaw

The ever-industrious Vince (Gareth Hunt) and his hapless neighbors Gilly (Louisa Rix) and Katie (Mia Fothergill). *BBC Worldwide*

This was a short-lived but thoroughly enjoyable series. Writer Richard Ommanney, creator of the earlier sitcom *Three Up, Two Down*, again has fun with the premise of conflicting characters living at exceptionally close proximity to each other. Here, two sets of suburban next-door neighbors—Gilly and her daughter Katie on one side of the fence, and Vince and wife Stella on the other—struggle to remain civil with each other despite numerous mishaps and annoyances on both sides. However, it is the well-meaning but rather tactless Vince who proves the major irritant to both Gilly and Stella.

The series opens at the funeral of Gilly's husband Robert, who died while having an affair with his secretary. As good neighbors, Vince and Stella attend the funeral, but Vince is not above handing out business cards (including one to the vicar) for his plumbing business. Vince has a history of unintentionally aggravating Gilly with everything from a squeaky weather vane on his chimney, to his long-standing request to allow him to add an unsightly extension to his house. In this opening episode, we are also introduced to Vince's pride and joy, still under construction in the front yard: a gaudy, oversized fountain complete with urinating cherubs.

One day Vince and Stella's sulky teenage nephew Terry arrives for a stay of undetermined length. He's been in danger of becoming a full-fledged hooligan, and is in need of a disciplined routine. Vince reluctantly takes him on as his plumber's assistant. As soon as Terry and Katie meet, a mutual attraction is established, although Katie decides to take the phrase "playing hard to get" to new heights.

A few days after Robert's funeral, Gilly and Katie decide to scatter his ashes in the river he enjoyed. Despite their lingering bitterness towards him, they decide it's the right thing to do.

Meanwhile, Vince is next door swinging a pickax in the hole he is digging for his fountain. Gilly and Katie have just stepped outside with Robert's urn when Vince strikes a water main. The resulting geyser drenches Gilly as the urn slips out of her hands, scattering the ashes on the driveway. Vince's usual reaction is to shrug, smile, and offer Gilly a hand in getting up.

In another episode, Vince has enlisted Terry and Katie to help him erect a forty-foot windmill in his backyard. It's for the sake of the environment, he reasons with Gilly, who is horrified at the size of the structure. Once the frame is pulled into an upright position, Vince is encouraged by the proud Stella and Terry. He unlocks the propeller brake as they all watch a strong gust of wind send the blades rotating out of control. The entire windmill frame shakes itself loose and comes crashing down on Gilly's greenhouse. She stands there fuming as Vince apologizes. He adds the unhelpful words, "I didn't say saving the planet was going to be easy."

While Louisa Rix has also been seen in the Britcom role of Jen in *Colin's Sandwich*, Gareth Hunt is known to cult television enthusiasts for his 1976-77 role in *The New Avengers* (with Joanna Lumley and Patrick MacNee).

ABSOLUTELY FABULOUS

BBC
1992-1995
18 Episodes

With best friend Patsy (Joanna Lumley, *front right*), Edina (Jennifer Saunders, *front left*) continually tests the patience of her mother (June Whitfield) and daughter, Saffron (Julia Sawalha). *BBC Worldwide*

Written by Jennifer Saunders
Directed by Bob Spiers
Produced by Jon Plowman

Available on home video in the U.S.

Cast:

EDINA MONSOON	Jennifer Saunders
PATSY STONE	Joanna Lumley
SAFFRON	Julia Sawalha
BUBBLE	Jane Horrocks
MOTHER	June Whitfield

Absolutely Fabulous has received more attention and praise in America than perhaps any Britcom since *Fawlty Towers*. The attention is due mainly to the great deal of advanced hype by its U.S. carrier Comedy Central. The praise can be credited to the creativity of writer and actor Jennifer Saunders. The series' bawdy dialogue and perpetually inebriated and/or promiscuous lead characters Edina and Patsy may have shocked some at first (public television stations kept their distance from this one), but the majority of viewers and critics have embraced *AbFab*. It is a sitcom that throws a defiant attitude in the face of the political correctness movement.

Jennifer Saunders has been one of the top comedians in Britain since the early 1980s, when she first teamed with her rotund sidekick Dawn French. Together, French and Saunders achieved notoriety for their improvisation skills as well as for their written sketches. As members of The Comic Strip improvisation troupe, they found success on television (with fellow members Adrian Edmondson and

Rik Mayall) in 1982 with *The Comic Strip Presents* . . . in which they mostly lampooned film and TV styles. In 1985, they starred together with Tracy Ullman and American expatriate Ruby Wax in the sitcom *Girls on Top*. The following year, French and Saunders starred in their own innovative sketch series. One of those sketches, "Modern Mother and Daughter," later became the basis of Saunders's *Absolutely Fabulous*.

As for *AbFab* co-star Joanna Lumley, she has been a constant presence on British TV for over twenty years in both dramatic and comedic roles. She appeared in episodes of *Are You Being Served?* and other sitcoms, but also made a name for herself as co-star with Patrick MacNee in *The New Avengers*. She also appeared in the James Bond film *On Her Majesty's Secret Service* and teamed with David McCallum in the science-fantasy series *Sapphire and Steel* from 1979–82.

Absolutely Fabulous is many things other sitcoms probably wish they could be, but don't have the nerve. As with many other classic comedies, a typical episode doesn't spend inordinate time on plot. Edina ("Eddy") and Patsy ("Pats") are so outlandish in their words and actions that they don't necessarily have to do much of anything plot-wise to make them worth watching. Sight gags, pratfalls, and other variations of slapstick abound, usually as a result of our heroines stumbling through their lives in a perpetually inebriated daze.

Eddy and Patsy are both peripheral players in the fashion world. Eddy is a fashion publicist during her fleeting moments of sobriety, while Patsy, who has even *fewer* moments of sobriety, edits a fashion magazine. They are both obsessed with celebrities and particularly enjoy engaging in catty comments about their glamorous female contemporaries, such as Ivana Trump, Joan Collins, and of course, Princess Diana.

When we first meet Eddy in the premiere episode "Fashion," she is waking up from her latest hangover. It's the day of a big fashion show for which she has to help organize. Dealing with responsibility is not her specialty. While still in bed, she cures a short-lived panic attack with a swig, but opening the bedroom curtains nearly blinds her. She stumbles downstairs to the kitchen, where her ever-studious daughter Saffy is alternately studying and giving her inebriated mother disapproving looks. We soon learn that despite Eddy's self-destructive habits, she regularly succumbs to weekly fads such as healing crystals, dream interpretation, and Buddhist chanting. In addition, her daily wardrobe consists of the most ghastly 1970s rejects imaginable. Poor Saffy is forever at the breaking point as her helpless mother routinely berates her one

moment and pleads for her help the next. Saffy rarely bothers to keep her frustrations to herself. "You live from self-induced crisis to self-induced crisis," she scolds her mother. "Someone chooses what you wear. Someone does your brain, someone tells you what to eat, and three times a week someone sticks a hose up your bum and flushes it all out of you." Eddy, unfazed, replies, "It's called colonic irrigation, darling, and it's not to be sniffed at."

Eddy's pal Patsy is perhaps the only other person on Earth in tune with Eddy's wavelength. A connoisseur of alcohol, cocaine, casual and often anonymous sex, Patsy's only redeeming feature is her loyal and steadfast friendship with Eddy—probably because no level-headed person would want to be friends with either one of them. While recalling the time when she was supposedly going out with Keith Moon, she modifies the claim, "Well, sort of. I woke up underneath him in a hotel bedroom once." Patsy also despises Saffy for being uptight, judgmental, and for usually getting in the way of a good time. Eddy rarely bothers to defend her daughter, who returns Patsy's contempt with equal vigor.

Curiously, Jennifer Saunders has expressed no qualms about creating characters with such undesirable, even vile, personality traits. "I try and make everybody as negative as possible," she told *TV Guide*, "I can't see the point of a positive character." Saunders and Lumley appeared on *60 Minutes* in 1995 for a conversation with correspondent Morley Safer (the last reporter most people would think of to host a story on *AbFab*). Saunders reiterated her assessment of Eddy and Patsy: "I've compacted every vice into these two people . . . they're revolting people . . . they're pretty awful. I try to make them worse and worse only because I find [that] people like them too much!"

Despite the fact that Eddy and Patsy's friendship is the flashy focal point of the show, Saunders sees the series as being as much about Eddy's relationship with Saffy, who is the closest thing to a positive character on the show. Mother and daughter have been living in reversed roles probably since Saffy could speak. Saffy is smart, logical, and responsible while her mother is spoiled, hedonistic, and chronically self-absorbed. Saffy even has to act as disciplinarian when Eddy's antics go over the line. This situation is highlighted in the episode

Two of a kind: Eddy and Patsy. *BBC Worldwide*

"Forty" in which Eddy's fortieth birthday causes all sorts of distress throughout the household.

Eddy is determined to spend her birthday in even greater misery than usual. "It's like I've hit an oil patch at thirty-five and I'm skidding toward the grave, darling," she whines to Saffy. Saffy offers a birthday present but no sympathy, although she announces her planned luncheon in Eddy's honor. The guest list includes Eddy's mother, Patsy, and both of Eddy's ex-husbands. When Eddy's complaints about the guests (and everything else) steamroll into mean-spirited rantings, Saffy slaps her across the face. Eddy stands there, shocked. "That's illegal, isn't it?" she whimpers. Saffy sends her mother upstairs to prepare for the guests.

The guests soon arrive. One of Eddy's ex-husbands, Marshall (played by *The Young Ones* alumnus Christopher Ryan), is in a fragile state recovering from drug and alcohol abuse. He is now with a flaky, pampering Californian woman who leads him around by the hand and spoon-feeds his restricted diet to him. Eddy's other ex, Justin, is accompanied by his gay partner Oliver. Eddy sneaks to the top of the kitchen stairs to spy on the guests, but makes an inelegant entrance by tripping and sliding down the stairs headfirst. It's not long before she finds a way to alienate each and every one of her guests (except Patsy, of course). A particularly fierce spat with Oliver concludes with his remark, "I see no point in celebrating the fact that she's lived so bloody long!" After sharing a marijuana joint in the upstairs bathroom, Eddy and Patsy return to the kitchen for the birthday cake.

Unnerved by the number of candles atop the cake, Eddy brings the celebration to a halt by putting them out with a fire extinguisher. The proceedings later crumble even further into anarchy as the two pals dance on the table tops, singing karaoke-style to old rock songs (including the *AbFab* theme).

Eddy and Patsy's more outlandish adventures have taken them abroad on occasion. In Morocco, they embark on a shopping spree, manage to offend the locals, and actually sell Saffy for a handsome profit. In France, Eddy and Patsy mistake a dilapidated farmhouse for their reserved luxury chateau. New York becomes Eddy's spur-of-the-moment shopping destination when she decides to search for a particular style of doorknob.

Absolutely Fabulous has won the BAFTA Award for best comedy, and Joanna Lumley's performance as Patsy has won her both a BAFTA and a 1994 Emmy (that same year, she also starred in the comedy-drama series *Class Act* written by *Waiting for God* author Michael Aitkens).

As a last hurrah, Saunders wrote a ninety-minute version of the show called *The Last Shout* which aired in Britain in the fall of 1996, and in the United States in January of 1997. Among the highlights are Eddy and Patsy's ski trip to the French Alps, where Eddy's near-fatal ski run brings her face to face with God (or is it Marianne Faithfull?). The story culminates with Saffy's impending wedding to a rich but heartless young snob. As usual, things don't turn out quite as planned. *The Last Shout* was a fitting sendoff for one of the silliest and most brazen Britcoms to come along in years.

Chef!

BBC
1993-1996
20 Episodes

(*Left to right*): Otto (Erkan Mustafa), Everton (Roger Griffiths), Gareth (Lenny Henry), Piers (Gary Parker), and Lucinda (Claire Skinner).

BBC Worldwide

Written by Peter Tilbury
Directed by John Birkin, Dewi Humphries
Produced by Charlie Hanson

Available on home video in the U.S.

Cast:

Gareth Blackstock	Lenny Henry
Janice Blackstock	Caroline Lee Johnson
Everton	Roger Griffiths
Lucinda	Claire Skinner
Lola	Elizabeth Bennett
Cyril Bryson	Dave Hill
Gustav	Jeff Nuttall
Savannah	Lorelei King
Otto	Erkan Mustafa
Piers	Gary Parker

Lenny Henry was an experienced comedian by the time he settled comfortably into this starring vehicle. He had burst onto the scene in 1975 as winner of the New Faces TV competition at the tender age of sixteen. In time, his popular and more than a little abusive comedy diatribes resulted in numerous appearances on variety specials such as *Comic Relief, The Secret Policeman's Third Ball*, and several TV specials of his own. He also starred with Tracy Ullman in the sketch series *Three of a Kind* (1981, 1983) and starred in his own short-lived *Lenny Henry Tonight* (1986), written by Ben Elton. This show was presented as a comic anthology of sorts, in which Henry portrayed a different character in a different situation each week. *The Lenny Henry Show* (1987–1988) gave him a chance to feature some of his more popular characters, including his own role as flamboyant disc jockey Delbert Wilkins.

Henry came up with the original idea of doing a series about a chef in the Caribbean district of London. Writer Tilbury did a good deal of research and decided, "I wanted him to be a driven, Michelin-cooking chef because they seem to be the 'sexy' ones." A composite of Britain's most notorious chefs was born—Gareth Blackstock, the owner and Chef de Cuisine of Le Chateau Anglais. He is a brilliant and dedicated chef but also a nasty, egomaniacal tyrant in the kitchen and everywhere else. By his own admission, Gareth is "seriously unpleasant. I am a bastard. My single aim in life is to send the finest, best presented food through that door. That's it! And if it is at the costs of a few human lives, then that's fine by me." His underlings—especially his soft-spoken, childhood friend Everton—suffer his verbal abuse and intimidation probably only out of their respect for his unflagging perfectionism and devotion to the culinary arts. There is only one person who could bring Gareth's rantings to an abrupt halt and with a scornfully raised eyebrow, reduce him to jelly. She is his beautiful wife and business manager Janice, who knows just how and when to set Gareth straight whenever his explosive personality threatens to muck things up at the restaurant.

One of the highlights of the series is the episode "England Expects." We begin a typical day in the kitchen, with Gareth bawling out an underling (this time it's his French wine steward Alphonse). Gareth then receives an invitation to a major cooking competition in Lyon, France—requiring him to sacrifice the two-week relaxation holiday Janice was hoping for. After a bit of wavering between his self-confidence and his perception of biased French judges, Gareth decides to prepare an English dish, using only English ingredients, including the wine. A baffled Alphonse leads them to a winery where they finally find an acceptable English wine. Marathon practice preparations follow. On the day of their flight to Paris, Gareth and Everton even reserve a third airplane seat for their packages of ingredients to ensure tender loving care.

Once in Lyon, the duo arrives in the preparation hall and are met with glares and sarcastic comments by the chefs from the other countries. A French competitor, Gaston, is particularly irksome to the British chefs. Before long, they discover the remainder of their wine is missing, and suspect Gaston, but can't prove it. They find the nearest

Crisis in the kitchen. Gareth's colleagues would be wise to duck for cover as Chef's temper reaches the boiling point. (*Left to right*): **Everton (Roger Griffiths), Lucinda (Claire Skinner), Gareth (Lenny Henry), and Lola (Elizabeth Bennett).** *BBC Worldwide*

winery but their request for an English wine is met with laughter by the clerks in the wine cellar. Luckily, Janice has already thought to bring an extra bottle with her on Competition Day. Gareth is so grateful to her that his unfamiliar gushing words of praise make her wish he were back to his normal self. Later, the prizes are awarded, and after receiving two second place trophies and a third place award, the disappointed Gareth actually wins the grand prize. Gaston offers his congratulations and asks that they exchange hats. Gareth still suspects the Frenchman as the wine thief, but upon lifting his own hat as it stands upright on the counter, he inadvertently reveals the original missing bottle. He sheepishly offers the bottle to Gaston, saying, "I hope you like it. It's quite difficult to get a hold of in France."

The third series brought changes both in front of and behind the camera. Geoff Deane and Paul Makin took over the writing, and the episodes were now shot on video as opposed to film, and mostly in the studio in front of a live audience. There were also some changes made in the story and cast. The personal relationships between the lead characters began to take greater prominence over various culinary-related issues that were the thrust of the earlier series.

As the third series opens, Gareth's fortunes take a downturn as he loses ownership of the restaurant to loudmouthed businessman Cyril Bryson (Dave Hill). Gareth considers Cyril a culinary Philistine, so he manages to retain control over his kitchen and its staff members. The newest addition is brash American cook Savannah (Lorelei King).

Gareth's continuing obsession with the restaurant and with Cyril become more than Janice can take. She finally leaves him. Heartbroken and unable to win her back, Gareth delves even deeper into his work and reluctantly takes a few unsure steps into the social dating scene. But it is his own colleague Savannah who seems to have eyes for him. To complicate matters, Cyril harbors lustful desires for Savannah!

Throughout the series, real life chef Paul Headman received a "Food Preparation" credit for creating the authenticity of the many fascinating and detailed food preparation scenes in Gareth's kitchen.

THE DETECTIVES

BBC
1993-1994
12 Episodes

Written by Steve Knight and Mike Whitehill
Produced by Ed Bye

Cast:

BOB LOUIS .... Jasper Carrott
DAVE BRIGGS .... Robert Powell
SUPERINTENDENT COTTAM ..... George Sewell

Briggs (Robert Powell), Cottam (George Sewell), and Louis (Jasper Carrott), appearing more competent than they actually are. *BBC Worldwide*

The Detectives began as a series of sketches on Jasper Carrott's *Canned Carrott* program in 1990. Each week, the filmed segments shot on location would parody the gritty, urban detective dramas so prevalent on British TV. As director Ed Bye explained, "The big attraction for that was in order to pastiche it nicely we had to shoot on film. And that became a very popular part of the series, so we then developed that into a full-blown series of its own."

Undercover detectives Louis and Briggs effortlessly botch up each assignment they're given, and often find their own lives hanging in the balance, all the while never failing to blame each other for their predicaments. Somehow, they always manage to foil the criminals they've set out to catch.

In keeping with the original concept, many episodes of the series open with scenes fairly ominous in tone, much like familiar police dramas. In one opening scene, Louis and Briggs stand on a dock, watching somberly as a car is crane-lifted out of the Thames. It is brought to rest by their side. They look to each other and, with some hesitance, get in and attempt to start the car—revealing it is in fact *their* car, which, due to circumstances left to our imagination, ended up in the river.

"Teed Off" also opens with a touch of suspense, as two mysterious figures make their way through a darkened room with only their flashlights for guidance. Suddenly the lights switch on. It is Briggs and Louis, poking around in Louis's small, cluttered apartment. The flat had gone dark due to his obsolete (but economical) coin-operated light meter. Their ensuing chat leads them to discover that they're both going for the same promotion to Detective Sergeant. Suddenly competitive in both word and deed, they meet the following day in Superintendent Cottam's office. Their new

Briggs, Superintendent Cottam, and Louis, as the boss reluctantly trusts his detectives with a new assignment.
BBC Worldwide

assignment is to follow a powerful and dangerous arms dealer named McKenna as he plays a round of golf with an equally notorious Colombian drug dealer. McKenna prefers holding his meetings on the golf course to avoid being monitored, but Briggs and Louis are to stay close enough to use a special golf club containing a two-way radio in the club's head.

No sooner are both detectives on the course than they display their profound ignorance of the game's rules and protocols. To make their bumbling even more conspicuous, they've decided to use a motorized, remote-controlled cart for their golf bag. The cart proves a little too unwieldy to keep close at hand.

Unknown to the duo, McKenna's drug-dealing contact has been held at customs, so McKenna agrees to play with the club pro (played by British golf legend Tony Jacklin). Briggs and Louis bumble their way through the course, constantly making spectacles of themselves and distracting McKenna to the point where subtle threats are in order. Later, one of McKenna's thugs recognizes the two as detectives. McKenna has them brought upstairs in the clubhouse to find out what they know about the planned drug deal. He has Louis tied to the wall, tapes his mouth shut, and literally tees off at point-blank range. The golf shots come hideously close to Louis's most delicate area. Between tee shots, McKenna demands that Briggs come forth with the information. But Briggs, still bucking for a promotion and aware that Cottam is listening in, defiantly replies that he's not afraid of a little physical pain. McKenna turns to Louis and says, "I'm beginning to feel sorry for you. Your partner's bloody mad." Cottam, listening on the two-way radio, hears Briggs's defiance followed by Louis's muffled screams of fear, and believes it is Briggs who is undergoing the torture. Cottam's helpful young assistant, Williams, rightly points out that since McKenna's incriminating remarks have been caught on tape via the two-way radio, he can now be arrested. The other officers break into the room and rescue Louis and Briggs, but not before McKenna managed to get one last tee shot to Louis's crotch. Later, Cottam congratulates the team, but when Louis asks about the promotion, Cottam agrees that one is in order, and gives it to Williams.

"It worked very well," recalled director Ed Bye, "but I particularly liked it because it was shooting on film, which I hadn't had a great opportunity to do up until that point. And that was a series that *did* work well filmed and then played to an audience. They gave us forty days to do a series of six, which comes to three hours of cut film. It's quite tight. It was shot in a very rushed and rabid way. Nevertheless it was great fun."

GOODNIGHT SWEETHEART

**BBC
1993–
2 Series, 16 Episodes**

*Written by Laurence Marks and
Maurice Gran
Directed by Robin Nash*

Cast:

GARY SPARROW .... Nicholas Lyndhurst
YVONNE SPARROW .... Michelle Holmes
PHOEBE BANFORD .... Dervla Kirwan
ERIC BANFORD .... David Ryall
RON .... Victor McGuire
PC REG DEADMAN .... Christopher Ettridge

Back to the present: (*left to right*) Ron (Victor McGuire), Phoebe (Dervla Kirwan), Gary (Nicholas Lyndhurst), Yvonne (Michelle Holmes), and Reg (Christopher Ettridge).
BBC Worldwide

Few television series have boasted as imaginative a premise as that of *Goodnight Sweetheart*. A man in present-day London discovers he can step back in time to 1940 and return again as he chooses. It is a series that grows in complexity over time, and its charms tend to sneak up on the viewer almost without warning. *Dad's Army* notwithstanding, never has a Britcom import captured the atmosphere of wartime England with the authenticity and heart of *Goodnight Sweetheart*.

We first meet Gary Sparrow, a young television repairman married to a pretty but often cranky wife named Yvonne. Out on a job one day, Gary heads down a London alleyway called Ducketts Passage, and emerges at the other end in the early days of World War II during the Blitz, a time of air raids and ration books. Ignorant of this at first, Gary enters a pub to ask directions, and mistakes it for a "theme" pub. He finds the

authentic recreation of a wartime pub quite amusing. The pub owner, Eric, is a gruff, older man who doesn't appreciate Gary's jokes about the war and immediately harbors suspicions about him. It doesn't help that Gary has ordered a beer without having the wartime currency to pay for it, and worse, he's found to own a pen made in Germany! Eric accuses Gary of being a spy. His daughter Phoebe, working behind the bar, points out the silliness of the idea. Gary gets an uneasy feeling that all is not right. He steps outside to spot further evidence that he's either in 1940 or is having a dream. He decides to enjoy the dream, and concocts a story for Phoebe that he's been in America for some time, working as a songwriter (he entertains the patrons with modern day rock and pop songs, claiming to be the author). He also hints about his work as an agent for the American government, and blurts out that he has a girlfriend named Marilyn Monroe. Phoebe has a husband in the service in North Africa, but nonetheless finds herself attracted to Gary's worldly experience. A sudden air raid, with *real* bombs, convinces Gary that this is no dream. He really is in 1940, and even finds himself rescuing an unconscious Eric with mouth-to-mouth resuscitation. Gary is hailed as a lifesaver and hero, even though he can barely comprehend what's happening to him.

Gary discovers to his relief that he can return to the present day and go back again at will. The only person who knows of Gary's ability to step into the past is his friend Ron, who at one point attempts to join Gary for a stroll down that fateful alley. But he soon discovers that only Gary is destined to reach the other end.

The imaginative idea for the series came from Laurence Marks and Maurice Gran, one of the most successful writing teams in British television. Among their successes was an early 1980s sitcom *Shine on Harvey Moon*, set in the years just after WWII. "It was a period we were interested in," explained Gran, "and a period we knew quite a lot about . . . certainly that immediate post-war period interested us."

Some years after *Shine on Harvey Moon*, the team was writing a drama which included a scene set in a part of London that hasn't changed very much since the war. As Gran recalled, "Laurence said off-hand, 'Wouldn't it be interesting if there was a part of London which was locked into that period, where it was still the war?' And I said to him, 'That's probably a series.'"

Goodnight Sweetheart is presented in serial form. The continuing storyline brings about unforeseen complications for Gary as he begins to spend more time in wartime London with Phoebe. They quickly find themselves deeply attracted to each other, but his frequent and prolonged absences confuse and frustrate her. At one point in the story, Ron convinces Gary that a wise investment made in the early 1940s could reap untold financial awards upon collection in the 1990s. Gary returns to the wartime period and proceeds to a bank manager's office, where he soon comes face-to-face with the manager, a balding, bespectacled man named Mainwaring, whose tall, slow-moving assistant is named Wilson. Gary "recognizes" them immediately, and can't help but have a laugh about it. The

Reg (Christopher Ettridge), Phoebe (Dervla Kirwan), and Gary (Nicholas Lyndhurst) trade opinions on the Blitz. *BBC Worldwide*

scene serves as a clever and hilarious inside joke for anyone familiar with the characters in the classic *Dad's Army*.

Returning to more serious matters at hand, Gary has fallen in love with Phoebe (whose father Eric has since been killed in an air raid), and finds himself getting increasingly tangled in his dual life. He knows he can't stay in 1940s London with her, but he can't bear to stay away, either. Back in the present day, Gary's wife Yvonne, who has noticed Gary's increasingly strange behavior, is determined nevertheless to fix their marriage, buy a house, and even start a family. A forlorn Gary wonders out loud to Ron, "How did I manage to simultaneously screw up two lives fifty-three years apart? I'd even consider suicide if I didn't think I'd have to do it twice."

As Maurice Gran explained, "Only later on did we realize to what an extent it was a show about adultery . . . [Gary] never pays the price in terms of discovery or comeuppance, because he's fireproof. But of course, the price for adultery or any sort of playing around is emotional strain." Gran believes the show has never been seriously criticized for its dubious moral fiber not only because its premise lies in fantasy, but because of its star. "When we first had the idea," he said, "we felt that there was only one possible actor to play him, and that was Nicholas Lyndhurst. And we felt that probably he was the only person who could neutralize the moral question. . . . We got together with him really before we'd written anything."

As the story continues, life becomes increasingly complicated for Gary. He concludes that he must, once and for all, go back to Phoebe permanently, never to return to the present. He fakes his suicide by leaving his clothes and a suicide note on a bridge. He says good-bye to Ron (who's in on the plan) and returns to 1941, where he rents an apartment near Phoebe's pub. Taking up permanent residence obligates Gary to become a true member of the community. He's asked to participate in the nightly civilian fire watches, during which those on duty must scramble to put out small fires left by German incendiary bombs. The prospect frightens Gary, who appears in the pub the next day with a sudden limp and equally lame excuse. The dreariness of life in wartime gets to him after a few days and he skulks back to the present and finds Ron, who isn't at all surprised to see him. It turns out that Gary's suicide note was never found, and

Yvonne thinks he's been away on business. Free to return home, Gary stays overnight.

Upon his reappearance in 1941 the next day, Gary is met with disapproval for skipping out on his fire watch duty the previous night, and promises Phoebe to stand watch with her on a warehouse roof that evening. An air raid follows, sending the two of them scampering to smother small fires on the rooftop. The chaos of bombs, fires, smoke, and sirens make for a traumatic evening. Later that night, a pale and shaken Gary returns to Yvonne and the comforts of home, with the murmur of German bombers and wail of sirens still in his head. He has learned some hard lessons about the war's effect on the common Londoners fighting the Blitz, their heroism (especially Phoebe's), and his own cowardice. The trauma of the war causes him to once again rethink his plan of staying permanently in 1941.

THE VICAR OF DIBLEY

BBC
1994-
2 Series, 12 Episodes,
3 Specials

Written by Richard Curtis, Paul Mayhew-Archer, Kit Hasketh-Harvey
Produced by Jon Plowman, Sue Virtue

Available on home video in the U.S.

Cast:

Reverend Geraldine Granger	Dawn French
David Horton	Gary Waldhorn
Hugo Horton	James Fleet
Frank Pickle	John Bluthal
Alice Tinker	Emma Chambers
Mrs. Cropley	Liz Smith
Jim Trott	Trevor Peacock
Owen Newitt	Roger Lloyd-Pack

(*First row, left to right*): Hugo Horton (James Fleet), Alice (Emma Chambers), Reverend Geraldine (Dawn French), and David Horton (Gary Waldhorn). In the back row are Frank Pickle (John Bluthal), Jim Trott (Trevor Peacock), and Owen Newitt (Roger Lloyd-Pack).
BBC Worldwide

While Dawn French and Jennifer Saunders will probably be forever linked in the minds of most British comedy fans, they have proven that they each have the talent to succeed in their individual pursuits. Just as Saunders struck gold with *Absolutely Fabulous*, French has given us the appealing Reverend Geraldine Granger, the extroverted Vicar of Dibley.

The Vicar of Dibley (originally titled *The Village*) was created and principally written by the prolific Richard Curtis. His long list of credits include four series of *Not the Nine O'Clock News*, co-writer of the various *Black Adder* incarnations, *Mr. Bean*, and the films *Four Weddings and a Funeral* and *Notting Hill*.

The small rural town of Dibley has had the misfortune of witnessing its elderly vicar pass away in mid-sentence during a Sunday morning service. Actually, the church has not been attracting more than a handful of members for any one service for as long as most can remember. The town council, a motley crew headed by starchy David Horton, sends a request to the bishop for a replacement vicar. The council later meets on a rainy evening to await his arrival, only to be stunned when Geraldine appears at the doorstep to announce herself as their new vicar. She blows through the room with a big smile and rattles off racy jokes as she acquaints herself with everyone present. They stand with their jaws hanging to the floor. Most offended is David Horton, who considers the idea of a woman vicar to be simply unacceptable. He convenes a meeting the next day to draft a letter to the bishop, but Geraldine convinces the council to allow her the chance to lead a Sunday service before deciding. That Sunday, much to Horton's chagrin, the church is filled to capacity with congregation members who have come to marvel at the

Church sexton Alice (Emma Chambers, *left*)
and Reverend Geraldine (Dawn French, *right*)
are of the same mind regarding the pompous
David Horton (Gary Waldhorn), although
Alice's mind is usually on a time delay.

BBC Worldwide

Four more episodes of *The Vicar of Dibley* are
slated for 2000.

youthful, energetic, and most notably, female vicar.
And so, Geraldine's colorful tenure as the Vicar of
Dibley begins.

Series creator Richard Curtis never wanted to
write each episode himself. He sought out Paul
Mayhew-Archer to be his main collaborator. Curtis
would map out storylines, and the two would usually write episodes independently and then
exchange drafts for revisions. "*Dibley* was a very
happy experience," said Mayhew-Archer, "because
it's writing with somebody, even though we hardly
ever meet. It's just such a relief to have somebody
to bounce off." He also notes that the characters
have become bigger and more outrageous with
time. "Some writers have a complete bible of their
characters and their past, and they know everything
about them before they write the series. Certainly
in the case of myself and Richard on *Dibley*, we
don't know what happened to the characters
beforehand."

Dawn French won Top Television Comedy
Actress at the 1997 British Comedy Awards for
The Vicar of Dibley Christmas Special. In

November of 1998, the series won the International
Emmy for the episode featuring Hugo and Alice's
wedding. *The Vicar of Dibley* is actually the second
series in which Dawn French starred without comedy partner Jennifer Saunders. French starred in
three series of *Murder Most Horrid*, a detective
mystery-comedy (directed by *AbFab* director Bob
Spiers), plus occasional forays into TV films such as
Tender Loving Care and *Sex and Chocolate*. In
1996, she and Saunders also hosted, on alternate
weeks, *Dawn and Jennifer's Comedy Zone*, in
which they introduced their personal all-time
favorite sitcom episodes from both Britain and
America.

The creative people behind the cameras on
most of the programs starring the early 1980s generation of "alternative" comedians have also created
crisscrossing ties with each other. This family tree
continues to grow branches in every direction.

The Vicar of Dibley was directed by Dewi
Humphries, who not only directed French's
Murder Most Horrid, but also *Chef!*, starring
French's husband Lenny Henry.

Jon Plowman, producer of *The Vicar of
Dibley*, has served as producer for *Absolutely
Fabulous*, *French and Saunders*, *Fry and Laurie*,
and *Alas Smith and Jones*. In 1994, he was made
head of Comedy Entertainment at the BBC.

Sue Virtue has produced *The Vicar of Dibley*
as well as *Mr. Bean*, and has co-produced Comic
Relief. She first worked in various TV commercial
companies, then joined Tiger Television. Tiger and
Aspect films merged in 1993.

It's obvious that those in this comedy clique
work together well and know how to produce
superior comedy series. So, why tamper with
success?

NELSON'S COLUMN

BBC
1994-1995
12 Episodes

Written by Paul Mayhew-Archer
Produced by Susan Belbin

Cast:

GAVIN NELSON	John Gordon-Sinclair
CLARE	Sophie Thompson
MIKE	Steven O'Donnell
JACKIE	Elizabeth Counsell
LORRAINE	Camille Coduri

The day wouldn't be complete without Gavin (John Gordon-Sinclair) accomplishing a feat such as gluing a phone to his head. Clare (Sophie Thompson) knows how to take it in stride. *BBC Worldwide*

The amiable Scottish comic actor John Gordon-Sinclair has made a career of portraying somewhat hapless blokes. He first made a name for himself as the star of the charming 1980 comedy film *Gregory's Girl*, written and directed by Bill Forsyth (who also wrote and directed the film *Local Hero*, in which Sinclair had a smaller role). He had earlier starred in the sitcom *An Actor's Life for Me* (see *Short Takes*), and his collaboration with writer Paul Mayhew-Archer on that series continued with *Nelson's Column*.

In *Nelson's Column* Sinclair plays Gavin Nelson, a reporter for *The Herald*, a small town newspaper. Gavin, often accompanied by Mike the staff photographer, tends to bumble his way through the stories he covers, and even manages to create local headlines of his own.

As Mayhew-Archer recalled, once *An Actor's Life for Me* was canceled by the BBC Controller, "the head of BBC comedy at the time, Martin Fisher, said, 'You and John Gordon must do something else together.'" Susan Belbin, director of *One Foot in the Grave*, was also interested in working with Mayhew-Archer on a new project, but the writer had to struggle a bit before coming up with the idea for *Nelson's Column*.

As the first series begins, Gavin has a hopeless crush on fellow reporter Clare Priddy, but his awkward attempts at igniting a romance are quelled by her personal policy not to mix business with pleasure. He is not one to give up easily, however, and when he finds himself in need of a new apartment, decides to rent a flat in Clare's building. She is not amused. Unfortunately, Gavin strains their relationship even further by inadvertently assisting a couple of burglars in removing every stick of Clare's furniture from her flat!

Despite the setback, Clare finds herself attracted to Gavin, only to discover that she now has competition. Gavin has begun seeing Lorraine, a beautiful blonde with a pleasant personality but limited brain power. Their relationship becomes an on-again, off-again affair.

In "The Mousetrap," Gavin becomes the proud owner of his own house, although there is much work to be done to get it into decent shape.

After planting mouse droppings around in order to get a better price from the previous owners, he later discovers a real mouse has moved in with him as well. Meanwhile, at the office, demanding editor Jackie Spicer is suddenly in a wonderful mood, thanks to being in love. Lorraine, now Gavin's ex-girlfriend, visits him to complain about a terrible meal she had in a restaurant the previous evening. In her anger, she made a scene and declared that Gavin would expose all of the restaurant's offenses in his column. Mike, infatuated with Lorraine, tries to improve his hopelessly slim chances with her, and bribes Gavin and Clare to go on a double date. An evening of bowling ends with Mike getting his fingers stuck in a ball. Lorraine is not impressed.

The next day, Gavin finds a dead mouse in his toaster (which proves more efficient than his real mousetraps, as they tend to work only on his ear, fingers, etc.). He realizes he'll have a use for it later that day, when he takes Clare out to the restaurant Lorraine had complained about. Just as Lorraine had claimed, bad service and rude waiters are very much in evidence. With his dead mouse in tow, Gavin plants it on the dessert cart, intending to print a savage column the next day to hasten the restaurant's closing. As Jackie and her date Richard stop by to say hello, Gavin's complaints prompt Richard to turn and suddenly boss the staff around. Richard explains that he owns the restaurant. Before a mortified Gavin has time to react, another diner lets out a shriek—she has no doubt found the dessert containing the mouse.

In "Growing a Monster," Lorraine has entered a photo of herself in a crafts fair photography contest, and Gavin sneakily takes the judge's first prize ribbon from another entry and places it next to Lorraine's. His mischievous streak also leads to a brawl between two gardening contestants and soon innocent bystanders, including the photography judge, are sent to the hospital. Lorraine, Gavin, and Mike (who is experiencing double vision from looking at too many "Magic Eye" pictures) visit the photography judge in the recovery ward. The newly-confident Lorraine proceeds to take pictures throughout the hospital. Mike, meanwhile, is feeling decidedly threatened by the potential competition. Lorraine's enthusiasm for studying her photography books begins to take priority over her sex life with Gavin. "It's taking our relationship to a new level," she gushes. A frustrated Gavin replies, "Can't we go back to the old level for a bit?"

Meanwhile, Clare is having problems of her own, trying to get a story about a woman who is apparently keeping several goats in her flat. The woman also has a habit of pouring goat milk out of the second floor window onto the heads of nosy visitors, including Clare. For reasons made clear later, Clare uses the pen name "Barbara Whitworth" for her story (Gavin also uses the fake name on occasion, to give readers the impression of a larger editorial staff).

Later, Gavin questions the hospital administrator about reports of cotton swabs found in the patients' mashed potatoes. Mike and Lorraine both feel entitled to take photos for the story, but Mike wins out. He and Gavin later get into a scuffle about Lorraine in the hospital parking lot, just as another photographer from a rival paper snaps a picture of the two at each other's throats. As Lorraine gets lost trying to find her way out of the hospital, she discovers a woman patient who has been left unattended for days in an empty ward. Lorraine writes the story herself (also using the pen name Barbara Whitworth), which impresses Jackie enough to offer her a position at the paper. But the rookie's constructive criticism of the others' work puts everyone's nerves on edge. Gavin tries to scare her off, warning that being a journalist can be dangerous. Looking at their competitor's front-page photo of him and Mike angrily grappling each other, Lorraine replies, "The only person who's attacked you is your own photographer!" A short time later, the angry subject of Clare's goat story storms into the newsroom, demanding to see Barbara Whitworth. Lorraine offers that she's written under that name, and promptly receives a bucket of goat's milk poured over her head. She then calmly decides not to join the paper after all. "It's too risky."

"After the second series," said Paul Mayhew-Archer, "I got into a bit of a depression about writing alone. I decided I really didn't want to do any more of those!" His blues were soon relieved by the opportunity to collaborate with Richard Curtis on *The Vicar of Dibley*. In the meantime, John Gordon-Sinclair went on to star in a sitcom called *Loved by You*, Britain's version of the long-running American hit *Mad about You*.

Sophie Thompson (Clare) is the younger sister of the ubiquitous film actress and Academy Award winner Emma Thompson.

THE THIN BLUE LINE

BBC
1995–
2 Series, 13 Episodes,
1 Special

Written by Ben Elton
Produced by Ben Elton, Geoffrey Perkins
Directed by John Birkin

Available on home video in the U.S.

Cast:

INSPECTOR RAYMOND FOWLER ...	Rowan Atkinson
SERGEANT DAWKINS	Serena Evans
DETECTIVE CONSTABLE KRAY	Kevin Allen
POLICE CONSTABLE HABIB	Mina Anwar
POLICE CONSTABLE GOODY	James Dreyfus
POLICE CONSTABLE GLADSTONE ..	Rudolf Walker
DETECTIVE INSPECTOR GRIM	David Haig

Raymond (Atkinson, *center*) with his cohorts. *Clockwise from top*: Habib (Mina Anwar), Gladstone (Rudolf Walker), Grim (David Haig), Dawkins (Serena Evans), Kray (Kevin Allen), and Goody (James Dreyfus).
BBC Worldwide

Writer Ben Elton and actor Rowan Atkinson, former collaborators on the *Black Adder* series, team up again in a considerably more conventional sitcom set in a London metropolitan police station.

The Thin Blue Line is a long way from Elton's 1982 hit series *The Young Ones*, which just goes to show that even revolutionaries—in this case those in TV comedy such as Elton and Atkinson—inevitably tend to mellow with impending middle-age. However, the comedy here is still sharp. It's just a little more down-to-earth.

Elton drew upon his love of *Dad's Army* to create characters he wanted to be instantly familiar and popular with viewers. Atkinson plays Inspector Raymond Fowler, who oversees an eclectic squad of police constables. Raymond is an uptight sort who conducts his law enforcement strictly by the book. As Elton told the *Radio Times*, "Fowler is an old prig but he's a decent bloke. There's a Captain Mainwaring aspect about him." Fowler's coworkers give him little opportunity to enjoy much peace of mind. Sergeant Patricia Dawkins, for instance, also happens to be Raymond's live-in lover, and, despite being his subordinate on the job, openly speaks her mind whenever she has a bone to pick with him. Police Constable Gladstone hails from the Caribbean, and conflicts with Raymond's gung-ho attitude with a weary, sardonic counterpoint. The mildly effeminate Police Constable Goody prances about the police station suggesting flamboyance that out-Humphries the Mr. Humphries character in *Are You Being Served?* (although Goody has a crush of sorts for Habib). Detective Inspector Grim is the prickly perpetual thorn in Raymond's side, as he delights in mocking Raymond's ragtag squad of police constables, while boasting his own prowess in hunting down criminals. Fortunately for Raymond, Grim's hubris often proves his own undoing, leaving a smug Raymond to claim the ultimate moral victory.

The Thin Blue Line is well-represented by the episode "Rag Week." The title refers to the time-

(*Left to right*): Habib (Mina Anwar), Goody (James Dreyfus), and Gladstone (Rudolf Walker) report to an unamused Inspector Fowler (Rowan Atkinson).

BBC Worldwide

honored custom in which college students go out in public dressed in silly costumes and masks and pull various pranks to raise money for charity. Raymond and Grim agree that the students' behavior borders on public menace. For instance, a faxed note to the police station supposedly sent by an obscure terrorist organization comes as a welcome challenge to Grim, who hastily contacts every law enforcement agency in the country. However, Raymond deciphers the note to be a Rag Week prank, much to Grim's disappointment. Personal matters then come to the fore, as Patricia sends Raymond to the bank on his lunch hour to renew the standing orders for their television license. The absurdly long and slow lines, plus the unwelcome pestering from Police Constable Goody behind him, prove too much for Raymond's patience. He returns the station with his mission unfulfilled. The angry Patricia deems him to be a "bloody idiot," to which Raymond replies, "I'm not an idiot, I'm

your commanding officer. I'm only an idiot between one and two o'clock, after 6:30, and on weekends."

Grim brings in a group of students wearing gorilla masks and ballet tutus. Raymond admonishes them for bringing shame to Britain. "When Mr. Mitsubishi is asking himself 'Where shall I construct our new generation of small family hatchbacks?' do you think he's gonna say, 'Oh, I know, we'll go to Britain where the academic elite are a bunch of idiots in tutus and gorilla masks,' or will he go to Europe, where young people wear Benetton tops and respect authority?"

An attempted bank robbery brings Raymond and the squad to the scene. Patricia, doing Raymond's errand for him, is one of the hostages. During the standoff, the robbers demand a pizza delivery, but Raymond wants to speak to them. Grim tells him he's already tried all of his negotiating skills. Raymond retorts (in typical Ben Elton fashion), "You have the negotiating skills of an embittered Rottweiler. Your telephone manner is about as appealing as a pub toilet at closing time." After considerable debate among his underlings about which toppings should go on the pizza, Raymond disguises himself as the delivery boy and gains entrance to the bank. The robbers all happen to be wearing gorilla masks. Mistaking them for more Rag Week pranksters, Raymond berates them and identifies himself as a police officer. Patricia jumps up from the floor and does the same. The robbers panic. "Blimey, they're all coppers!" they blurt out, surrendering their weapons. Grim reluctantly thanks Raymond for a job well done. The grateful bank manager would like to do anything for Raymond and Patricia. She suggests they finally take care of renewing their standing orders. "Oh, I'm sorry, sir," the manager replies, "the bank closed three minutes ago."

PART IV

Short Takes

The following are Britcoms that have aired in the United States but for various reasons, simply did not enjoy much more than a brief visit to one or more PBS affiliates at any given time in the past twenty years.

Come Back, Mrs. Noah

BBC
1978
6 Episodes

Produced by David Croft
Written by Jeremy Lloyd and David Croft

Cast:

Mrs. Noah	Mollie Sugden
Clive Cunliffe	Ian Lavender
Carstair	Donald Hewlett
Fanshawe	Michael Knowles
Garstang	Joe Black
Mission Controller	Tim Barrett
Asst. Controller	Ann Michelle
Technician	Jennifer Lonsdale
TV Newscaster	Gorden Kaye

(*Left to right*): Carstair (Donald Hewlett), Mrs. Noah (Mollie Sugden), Clive (Ian Lavender), and Fanshawe (Michael Knowles) prepare for a simulated golf game aboard *Britannia 7*. *BBC Worldwide*

This slapstick-heavy series was written by the Croft/Lloyd team for Mollie Sugden, and was produced in between series of *Are You Being Served?*. Here she plays a housewife in the year 2050 who has won the opportunity to visit an orbiting space station, Britannia 7. Shortly after she and BBC reporter Clive Cunliffe arrive, a malfunction maroons all of the occupants, including the near-incompetent crew (Carstair, Fanshawe, and Garstang), 250 miles above the Earth on the wayward station. Back on the ground, Mission Control undertakes several unsuccessful rescue attempts.

Producer David Croft is known for having assembled an unofficial repertory company of comic actors in his twenty-five years in television, and he used them often throughout his many sitcoms. Several members of this Croft troupe star in *Come Back, Mrs. Noah*. Ian Lavender (Clive) had earlier been a regular cast member of *Dad's Army*. As reporter Cunliffe, Lavender assumes the role of Sugden's wisecracking foil, very similar to that of Mr. Lucas in *Are You Being Served?*. Michael Knowles (Fanshawe) co-wrote several *Are You Being Served?* episodes, as well as appearing in *You Rang, M'Lord?*. Gorden Kaye, seen here as the newscaster opening each episode with updates, was still a few years away from his starring role as Rene in Croft's *'Allo, 'Allo!*.

In addition to the usual Croft/Lloyd double entendres sprinkled liberally throughout the dialogue, most of the comedy revolves around Sugden tangling with various mechanical gadgets and devices in the space station. In the station's galley, she and the others encounter an automatic egg-laying device shaped liked a mechanical hen, which propels eggs across the counter at unpredictable speeds. Other space-age devices include pneumatic vacuum tubes for quick transport around the station, and a toilet mounted halfway up the bathroom wall, for when the station is tilted at the proper angle for use. The visual effects were supervised by Tony Harding. David Croft recalled, "Jeremy and I thought [*Come Back, Mrs. Noah*] was one of the funniest things we ever wrote. We had wonderful props made for us by the special effects department. We only wrote six. It was great fun."

ONLY WHEN I LAUGH

LWT
1979-1981
41 Episodes

Produced by Vernon Lawrence
Written by Eric Chappell

Cast:

ROY FIGGIS	James Bolam
ARCHIE GLOVER	Peter Bowles
NORMAN	Christopher Strauli
DR. THORPE	Richard Wilson
GUPTE	Derek Branche

The enjoyable and successful *Only When I Laugh* reached number one in the ratings in Britain, thanks to considerable talent on both sides of the camera. It is set in a hospital ward, where three recovering patients manage to create general havoc on the hospital floor. The ringleader is Roy Figgis, a hypochondriac and interfering busybody and perpetual source of angst for Dr. Thorpe. A typical episode has Figgis overhearing Thorpe on the phone, talking to a vet about his dog's poor health. Figgis assumes the subject of the conversation is himself. Being the uptight soul that he is, Figgis overreacts to what he hears and saddles the others with his misery.

The cast consisted of familiar faces to British audiences. James Bolam starred in a popular 1960s sitcom called *The Likely Lads*. Peter Bowles, of course, starred in *To The Manor Born*, *The Bounder*, and *Executive Stress*, as well as the comedy-dramas *Irish RM* and *Rumpole of the Bailey*. Richard Wilson later appeared in the sitcoms *Hot Metal*, and, as his crowning achievement in television comedy, *One Foot in the Grave*.

Prolific series creator/writer Eric Chappell has also written such superior sitcoms as *Rising Damp* and *The Bounder*.

AGONY

**LWT
1979-81
27 Episodes**

*Produced and directed by John Reardon
Written by Len Richmond and Anna
        Raeburn (series 1)
Stan Hey and Andrew Nickolds*

Cast:

JANE LUCAS . . . . Maureen Lipman
LAURANCE . . . . Simon Williams
BEA . . . . Maria Charles
DIANA . . . . Jan Holden

Real-life agony aunt Anna Raeburn collaborated with writer Len Richmond to create this series starring Maureen Lipman, an appealing actress skillful at light comedy. Lipman plays Jane Lucas, an agony aunt (advice columnist) for *Person* magazine. Jane is also host of her own radio call-in show, and when she isn't trying to solve the problems of her loyal readers and listeners, she must confront some heady personal problems of her own.

Jane is Jewish (as is Lipman)—a rarity for a Britcom—and is married to her WASPish husband, Laurance. As universal sitcom law apparently dictates, Jane must endure the meddling of her well-intentioned but nosy Jewish mother, Bea, played to the hilt by Maria Charles.

As the series progresses, Jane has a baby boy, for whom she arranges the traditional Jewish Bris ceremony, much to the resentment of Laurance's achingly conservative parents.

In 1995, *Agony* was revived as a new series, called *Agony Again*. Lipman happily resumed her role as Jane, now the host of a television talk show. Williams and Maria Charles also returned to the series.

SOLO

BBC
1981-1982
13 Episodes

Produced by Gareth Gwenlan
Written by Carla Lane

Cast:

GEMMA PALMER	Felicity Kendal
DANNY	Stephen Moore
GLORIA	Susan Bishop
MRS. PALMER	Elspet Gray

Exiled boyfriend Danny (Stephen Moore) and Gemma (Felicity Kendal) in happier times. *BBC Worldwide*

Felicity Kendal will forever be the adorable Barbara Good in *Good Neighbors* in the hearts of Britcom fans. Here she plays Gemma, a thirty-year-old who upon discovering her boyfriend Danny's affair with her best friend Gloria, has decided to move on with her life without either of them. Danny's indiscretion has left Gemma rather bitter towards men in general. Her widowed mother, who prefers to date men about twenty years her junior, is forever encouraging Gemma to start dating again (and to pay more attention to her biological clock). Danny reappears regularly in his futile attempts to patch things up with Gemma. He comes close on occasion, despite being a decidedly obnoxious fellow,

only to have Gemma pull the plug on the prospect of any rekindled romance.

Series creator/writer Carla Lane, author of *Butterflies* (and who has since created several popular comedy/drama series), tends to delight in using a sledgehammer for the male bashing she writes into her *Solo* scripts. Consequently, Gemma's resolve to start her life anew, and without men, fails to mask her rather unappealing bitterness.

Kendal and Lane later teamed up for a series called *The Mistress*, in which Kendal played the title role. Stephen Moore plays an amusing role in the feature film *Clockwise*, starring John Cleese.

EVER DECREASING CIRCLES

BBC
1984-1989
27 Episodes

Produced by Sydney Lotterby, Harold Snoad
Written by John Esmonde and Bob Larbey

Cast:

MARTIN BRYCE .... Richard Briers
ANN BRYCE .... Penelope Wilton
PAUL RYMAN .... Peter Egan
HOWARD .... Stanley Lebor
HILDA .... Geraldine Newman

First row, left to right: Martin (Richard Briers), Ann (Penelope Wilton), Paul (Peter Egan). *Back row*: Hilda (Geraldine Newman) and Howard (Stanley Lebor).
BBC Worldwide

Martin Bryce, a maddeningly efficient civic-minded citizen, thrives on juggling his duties between a dozen different clubs and organizations. His wife Ann barely tolerates his non-stop schedule of meetings and community activities, which he oversees from his cluttered, makeshift office in their home. Ann doesn't appreciate taking a back seat to her husband's well-meaning but obsessive social calendar. Martin does sit up and take notice, however, when Paul, an attractive, suave hair salon owner, moves onto the street. Something about Paul immediately rubs Martin the wrong way. Likewise, Paul considers Martin a bit of an oaf, and quietly delights in rankling Martin ("taking the Mickey" as the British say), usually with quietly sarcastic comments and an infuriating smirk on his face. More ominously, however, Paul seems to have his eye on Ann, who finds his attention and smooth ways more than a little refreshing.

Richard Briers, best known as Tom Good in *Good Neighbors*, has always been fun to watch regardless of his surroundings. *Ever Decreasing Circles* proved to have a little more staying power than another of his 1980s sitcoms, *All in Good Faith*. Briers recalled, "I liked that part very much because it was a character part, whereas with Tom Good I was almost playing myself, but Martin was a wonderful character because he was so unbearable." *Cult TV* magazine praised the series' pokes at middle-class values, describing the show as "criminally underrated."

HILARY

BBC
1985
12 Episodes

Produced by Harold Snoad
Written by Peter Robinson and Peter Vincent

Cast:

HILARY MYERS .... Marti Caine
GEORGE .... Philip Madoc
KIM .... Jack Smethurst
WESLEY .... Philip Fox
LYN .... Carolyn Moody

(*Left to right*): George (Philip Madoc), Hilary (Marti Caine), and Kim (Jack Smethurst).
BBC Worldwide

Hilary mixes *I Love Lucy*'s comic absurdity with *The Mary Tyler Moore Show*'s setting and cast of characters. The enjoyable, self-effacing performance of comedian Marti Caine provides *Hilary* with its strongest facet.

Hilary Myers is a tall, lanky, accident-prone researcher for the television interview program *Searchlight*. The program's producer, George, tends to scowl his way through the workday. He is forever exasperated by Hilary's disasters in the office, usually due to her long, awkward limbs. In the first episode alone (which is full of snappy lines), she accidentally knocks a tray of his papers to the floor and later knocks a mug of coffee onto his pants with her typewriter carriage. Hilary's wisecracking office colleague, Kimberley, is a middle-aged bachelor who speaks in one-liners to mask his fancy for her. On a rare occasion when Hilary arrives at work on time, Kim responds

with, "Go away, Hilary, you're not late yet." Another worker, Angela, is a haughty and prim type, and is forever casting a disapproving eye in Hilary's direction.

At home, the divorced Hilary lives with her minah bird Arthur, who has taught himself to say "knickers" whenever the phone rings. She shares a small apartment building with her pudgy, man-hungry friend Lyn and another neighbor, the timid young Wesley, who seems to live in slow motion, moans his words, and would be the hands-down winner in any low self-esteem contest.

Hilary's escapades range from work-related adventures, such as going to extremes to secure a television interview with a difficult American stunt man, to personal missions, such as seeking a vet in the middle of the night to care for a sickly Arthur.

Sadly, Marti Caine died of cancer at age fifty in November of 1995.

AN ACTOR'S LIFE FOR ME

BBC
1991
6 Episodes

Produced by Bryan Izzard
Written by Paul Mayhew-Archer

Cast:

ROBERT NEILSON . . . . John Gordon-Sinclair
DESMOND SHAW . . . . Victor Spinetti
SUE BISHOP . . . . Gina McKee

This series has had an unusual broadcast history. It began on BBC radio, moved to television for a brief stay, and then returned to radio. Creator Paul Mayhew-Archer explained, "I was working as a radio producer, and thought I'd have a go at a sitcom. We'd done a pilot with Nicholas Lyndhurst, who was too busy with other projects to do the series. We then re-cast it with John Gordon-Sinclair. We did two series on radio and a series on television." The program then returned to radio due to mediocre TV ratings, plus a BBC Controller who didn't particularly like shows about actors and entertainers. However, *An Actor's Life* had its admirers on the creative side of the business, such as director Susan Belbin (*One Foot in the Grave*) and writer Richard Curtis (*The Black Adder, The Vicar of Dibley*), both of whom later worked with Mayhew-Archer.

John Gordon-Sinclair plays Robert Neilson, a struggling young actor who finds himself with little choice but to take some of the most humiliating acting roles in the business. His agent, Desmond Shaw, maintains an upbeat, energetic

attitude regardless of Robert's frequent discouragement. It's easy for Desmond, who only has to send Robert to auditions with a pat on the back and big smile. In one episode, Robert agrees to take a role as a chauffeur in an action film, which requires him to undertake dangerous stunts involving scuba diving and rock climbing. Following Desmond's earlier advice, Robert assures the director that he can handle the physical stunts easily, concealing the fact that he not only bruises easily, but can't drive and has absolutely no stunt experience. His efforts for the film only succeed in landing him in the hospital.

Robert lives with his girlfriend Sue, a schoolteacher who sympathizes with Robert's struggles, but who sometimes gets weary of Robert's professional setbacks and intermittent income.

The presence of the wonderful veteran comic actor Victor Spinetti as Desmond is a welcome treat. Spinetti's career on TV and film dates to the early 1960s. He is perhaps most recognizable for his featured roles in the Beatles' films *A Hard Day's Night* and *Help!*.

You Rang, M'Lord?

BBC
1990-1993
25 Episodes, 1 Special

Produced by David Croft
Written by Jimmy Perry and David Croft

Cast:

ALF STOKES .... Paul Shane
IVY .... Su Pollard
JAMES TWELVETREES .... Jeffrey Holland
LORD MELDRUM .... Donald Hewlett
TEDDY .... Michael Knowles
POPPY .... Susie Brann
CISSY .... Catherine Rabett
LADY LAVENDER .... Mavis Pugh
MRS. LIPTON .... Brenda Cowling
HENRY .... Perry Benson
MABEL .... Barbara New
POLICE CONSTABLE WILSON ... Bill Pertwee

(*Left to right*): Ivy (Su Pollard), Alf (Paul Shane), and James (Jeffrey Holland). *BBC Worldwide*

Essentially a comic version of the classic serial *Upstairs, Downstairs*, this series (with fifty-minute episodes rather than the usual thirty or thirty-five minutes) features three actors from the long-running David Croft sitcom *Hi-De-Hi*: Paul Shane, Jeffrey Holland, and Su Pollard.

This 1920s period piece is set in Lord Meldrum's mansion, where he lives with his eccentric family. His brother Teddy is a spoiled layabout who tends to get mixed up in scandalous love affairs; Cissy is a stunning blonde who insists on wearing only men's clothes; and Meldrum's bedridden mother, Lady Lavender, has a habit of throwing food from her breakfast tray at whoever dares enter her bedroom.

The staff of hired help is headed by James Twelvetrees, a humorless, ever-so-proper butler who insists that even the slightest of protocols be strictly observed by the staff. His uptight manner

tends to get up the nose of fellow butler Alf, who at one point labels James (to his face, no less) "a pompous, stuck-up prig." Alf, meanwhile, must be careful to conceal from the family that Ivy the maid is in fact his own daughter, and one without proper professional experience. The naive Ivy barely manages to bumble her way through each day, and is only vaguely aware of the dubious goings-on in the household. The cook, Mrs. Lipton, has made the kitchen her own, and uses it as a haven where the staff can share their meals and gossip about their employers. They are visited regularly by Police Constable Wilson, who can never turn down one of Mrs. Lipton's dishes.

In addition to casting *Hi-De-Hi* veterans Shane, Holland, and Pollard for *You Rang, M'Lord?*, producer David Croft again exercises his proclivity for "recycling" his favorite comic actors from his many past creations. Here he has brought back Donald Hewlett and Michael Knowles from *Come Back, Mrs. Noah*, and Bill Pertwee from Croft's first major success, *Dad's Army.*

Actors Shane, Holland, and Pollard teamed up yet again for Croft in his 1996 sitcom *Oh, Doctor Beeching!* That series, set in the 1960s, centers on a small, rural railroad, struggling to survive the modern age and threat of corporate takeover. It is interesting to note again that among all of Croft's sitcoms, *Are You Being Served?* is the only one to have taken place in the present day, confirming that, with a healthy imagination, a writer can find ample comic fodder in looking back to days gone by.

Transatlantic Trauma: American Versions of Britcoms Don't Measure Up

There have been several occasions in which a British sitcom develops such a sterling reputation in Britain, and perhaps in the states as well, that an American producer or network will pay homage by attempting to recreate that success with an American version of the show. The odds against success are great. Rather than allowing Americans to be content with the laughter and joy so many brilliant Britcoms have brought us, Hollywood insists on watering down true comedy masterpieces with versions that often miss the point of the originals.

Let's go back to the early 1970s and, curiously enough, to an exception to the above. When Norman Lear adapted the British *Till Death Us Do Part* to create *All in the Family*, he launched the most influential and arguably one of the funniest American sitcoms in history. It is difficult to imagine even the British original achieving the depth of the characters (not to mention the groundbreaking content and language) of *All in the Family*. Lear achieved further success by transforming the British *Steptoe and Son* into *Sanford and Son*.

But how has the record of transatlantic transformations been since then? *Man about the House*, created by John Esmonde and Bob Larbey (*Good Neighbors*), is about two young women sharing a flat with a young guy, and became *Three's Company* here. While never known for its wit, *Three's Company* did get its fair share of laughs, mostly from John Ritter's talents as a slapstick comedian. However, the contrivance of passing himself off as gay in order to pacify the landlord Mr. Roper was not used in the original *Man about the House*, and was no doubt a product of American sitcom sensibilities in the late 1970s. *Three's Company* did follow its British counterpart

by producing a spinoff, *The Ropers* (*George and Mildred* in Britain). The comedy of *The Ropers* consisted in large part of familiar husband-wife put-downs, and was more depressing than funny.

Porridge, starring Ronnie Barker (also of *Open All Hours* and *The Two Ronnies*), was a very popular Britcom in the mid-1970s. *Porridge* was set in a prison, and was adapted in America to become *On the Rocks* in 1975. Originally scheduled as a companion piece to *Barney Miller*, *On the Rocks* lasted a single season.

Ted Knight and Nancy Dussault starred in *Too Close for Comfort*, a rather run-of-the-mill sitcom based on the run-of-the-mill Britcom *Keep It in the Family*. Still, *Too Close for Comfort* can be considered a success of sorts. It aired for almost six years, first on ABC and then in syndication, until Knight's death in 1986.

Next we have an example of American producers tampering with a comedy masterpiece. *Fawlty Towers*, considered by many the pinnacle of modern British situation comedy, somehow became *Amanda's* on ABC for half a season in 1983. Both series were set in a small hotel, both featured an incompetent Spanish waiter, and yet the creators of the American version eliminated Basil Fawlty from the mix. He instead became Amanda Cartwright, played by Bea Arthur (never known for her subtle delivery). Even if poor Basil had somehow survived this transatlantic crossing, there was no equivalent to John Cleese and Connie Booth's writing skills to be found in Hollywood. And, while scenes in *Amanda's* were indeed lifted from the original, it still begs the question: why? If viewers were expected to notice any kind of improvement over *Fawlty Towers*, they would be hard-pressed to find it. Logic dictates that no viewer would sit down and watch *Amanda's* when *Fawlty Towers* is hovering around nearby on a PBS affiliate.

Also in 1983, an attempt to adapt *The Fall and Rise of Reginald Perrin* resulted in *Reggie*, starring Richard Mulligan (*Soap, Empty Nest*). While Mulligan, like the late Leonard Rossiter, has his own arsenal of nervous tics and mannerisms, it is still difficult to envision a different face replacing the brilliant Rossiter who so deftly portrayed the harried businessman in the throes of a nervous breakdown. *Reggie* also managed to omit a significant development in the original series' storyline, in which Reggie Perrin fakes his own suicide to begin life anew and in disguise. The American *Reggie* lasted exactly one month.

The British *Dear John*, about a support group of divorcees, became *Dear John* in the U.S., with Judd Hirsch in the lead. The show had its merits, and lasted four years, but the nagging question still remains: why not bring the original here intact?

Next we have *Men Behaving Badly*. Premiering in Britain in 1992, audiences quite enjoyed being treated to a crude, slovenly duo who shared an apartment and had awful luck with women due to their boorish behavior. The American version a few years later (featuring *Saturday Night Live* alumnus Rob Schneider) was comparatively tame, and lasted only a season.

An American adaptation of *Are You Being Served?* failed to be picked up by U.S. television networks. (*Left to right*): Mr. Lucas (Trevor Bannister) expresses an unsolicited opinion to Mr. Granger (Arthur Brough), while Mr. Humphries (John Inman) keeps mum.

BBC Worldwide

Some American versions of British sitcom favorites never made it on the air, and perhaps that's just as well. In 1979, comedy director/producer Garry Marshall attempted to turn *Are You Being Served?* (which was still unseen here) into *The Beanes of Boston*. A pilot was shot, but the series didn't sell. More recently, in 1992 an American version of *Red Dwarf* came close to becoming a reality. As discussed in the *Red Dwarf* chapter, series creators/producers Rob Grant and Doug Naylor were allowed to act as creative consultants for the Hollywood version, but the pilot script proved to be in need of an overhaul. Several casting changes also took place (although Robert Llewellyn was prepared to leave the British version to continue his role as Kryten here). Problems grew, and in the end, the pilot failed to spark interest. UPN came up with *Homeboys in Outer Space* in 1996. This witless, juvenile *Red Dwarf* rip-off was put out of its misery later that season.

It can also be considered a blessing that Roseanne's plans to produce an American *Absolutely Fabulous* (starring Carrie Fisher) never got off the ground. The short-lived *AbFab* wannabe *High Society* starring Jean Smart and Mary McConnell showed potential in trying to emulate *AbFab*'s irreverence, but the critics were less than kind (as were the network execs who canceled it).

Maurice Gran, co-creator/writer of *Goodnight Sweetheart*, said, "When we pitched *Goodnight Sweetheart* in the states, there was a lot of enthusiasm for it, but also a lot of head scratchers, saying, 'Well, the trouble is, Americans don't understand history.' But we pitched it as a sort of Prohibition-era show, which I thought would work pretty well, and people said, sadly, 'Well, unfortunately, people don't remember that far back.'" It is sometimes difficult to tell, in a case such as this, whether American TV executives are accurately reflecting their audience's ignorance of history, and therefore can't accept a period sitcom, or if the executives themselves are merely demonstrating their own shortsightedness and lack of imagination.

Cosby, based ever-so-loosely on *One Foot in the Grave*, found success on CBS, no doubt due to the Cosby name. As it turns out, any similarities between this and the original series are purely coincidental. The sliver of resemblance is that both main characters are cranky, retired old men living at home. The early episodes of *Cosby* initially borrowed a good deal of material from *One Foot*, but the re-shot versions of the original scenes were somewhat limp by comparison. As Hilton Lucas, the ever-popular and cuddly Bill Cosby wouldn't allow himself to be *too* nasty, for fear that American audiences would reject the show. It would appear that the phrase "based on" is employed more for legal purposes than as creative acknowledgment. Missing from *Cosby*, naturally, are two elements that make the original *One Foot* the classic it is— the genius of David Renwick's writing and the remarkable innovation of Susan Belbin's direction.

Yet another ill-advised attempt to adapt *Fawlty Towers* to American sensibilities sprang up in March of 1999 with the series *Payne*, starring John Larroquette and JoBeth Williams. Curiously, John Cleese and Connie Booth sold their original scripts and characters to CBS the previous year for a substantial sum (although they did not relinquish the series' name). It might be considered a step in the right direction that this version at least retains a Basil Fawlty-like character, as opposed to his removal in *Amanda's*. John Larroquette is a skilled comic actor, albeit not one known for running about in the manic behavior perfected by Cleese. The effect of seeing a hotel lobby closely resembling that of the familiar hotel yet populated by different faces is rather eerie, as if it exists in some kind of parallel universe. The result is a program that's sort of like *Fawlty Towers*, but simply isn't.

To be fair, British TV has tried to recreate some American successes as well. *The Golden Girls*, wildly popular in Britain, became very briefly *Brighton Belles*. A pilot episode premiered on *Comedy Playhouse* in March of 1993, but the initial six-episode run later that year was canceled before all of the episodes aired. Carla Lane, who was appalled a decade earlier by the plans American TV executives once had for her own series *Butterflies*, has perhaps come to learn with *Brighton Belles* that such adaptations, no matter how sincere the effort (or how much potential money there is to be made), inevitably lose too much of their very essence in the transatlantic transition to justify the undertaking.

Cosby based its premise on *One Foot in the Grave*, but you would hardly know it. Richard Wilson played the original, and irascible, Victor Meldrew. *BBC Worldwide*

Still, the practice continues. One of the top American sitcoms of the 1990s, *Mad about You*, has been transformed, more or less, into the British *Loved by You* (starring John Gordon-Sinclair). Of course, Paul Reiser's comic vision and delivery aren't easy to get across without Paul Reiser, and Helen Hunt has proven herself to be equally irreplaceable. Also, picturing *Mad about You* without its unbilled co-star, New York City, proves a tough challenge.

Our lesson? The same holds true when trying to adapt sitcoms going in either direction and for either culture across the Atlantic—the odds for success are not in anyone's favor.

BRITCOMS ON VIDEO

Many Britcom fans may have heard about particular programs but have not had a chance to see them, depending on the Britcom purchase selections made by their local PBS affiliates. However, there is still a way to enjoy most of the programs featured in this book. CBS/Fox Video in association with BBC Video has released a steady stream of Britcoms on video in recent years. Most of the tapes listed below contain three episodes each. They are available at most quality video/music stores such as Suncoast Video and Tower Records, and at some major bookstore chains such as Borders.

The following series are available on CBS/Fox Video (except where noted):

SERIES	VOLUME TITLE
Absolutely Fabulous (available as box set)	Series 1, Part 1
	Series 1, Part 2
	Series 2, Part 1
	Series 2, Part 2
	Series 3, Part 1
	Series 3, Part 2
Are You Being Served?	Dear Sexy Knickers
	Big Brother
	German Week
	Wedding Bells
	Fifty Years On
	Happy Reunions
	Mrs. Slocombe Expects
As Time Goes By	Volume 1
	Volume 2

SERIES	VOLUME TITLE
The Black Adder (available as box set)	Black Adder 1, Part 1
	Black Adder 1, Part 2
	Black Adder II, Part 1
	Black Adder II, Part 2
	Blackadder the Third, Part 1
	Blackadder the Third, Part 2
	Blackadder Goes Forth, Part 1
	Blackadder Goes Forth, Part 2
	Blackadder's Christmas Carol
Bless Me, Father (Acorn Media)	Box set only, tapes 1-3
Butterflies (BFS Video)	
Chef!	Volume 1
	Volume 2: A Second Helping
Dad's Army (BFS Video)	The Day the Balloon Went Up
	Asleep in the Deep
	Two and a Half Feathers
	Deadly Attachment
	Big Guns
	Mum's Army
The Fall and Rise of Reginald Perrin (box sets, three tapes each, BBC/BFS Video)	Volume 1: The Beginning
	Volume 2: The Next Bit

SERIES	VOLUME TITLE	SERIES	VOLUME TITLE
Fawlty Towers (available as box set)	Germans The Psychiatrist The Kipper and the Corpse Basil the Rat		Smeg-Ups (outtakes) Red Dwarf VI—Gunmen of the Apocalypse Red Dwarf VI—Polymorph II/Emohawk Red Dwarf VII (Volume 1) (Volume 2) (Volume 3) Red Dwarf VIII (Volume 1) (Volume 2) (Volume 3)
Good Neighbors or The Good Life	Good Neighbors (Volume 1) Volume 2 Volume 3		
Hi-De-Hi	Hi-De-Hi		
Keeping up Appearances	How to Enhance . . . Rural Retreat Memoirs of Hyacinth Bucket Sea Fever I'm Often Mistaken . . . Angel Gabriel Blue My Family in Broad Daylight Entertaining the Hyacinth Way	Rising Damp (available in box sets, BFS Video)	Under the Influence Christmas Special
		The Thin Blue Line (Polygram Video)	Volume 1 Volume 2 Volume 3 Volume 4
Last of the Summer Wine (box set, BFS Video)		To The Manor Born	Volume 1 Volume 2 Volume 3 Volume 4
One Foot in the Grave	In Luton Airport . . . Who Will Buy?	The Vicar of Dibley	The New Girl in Town My Congregation . . . The Specials Love is in the Air
Open All Hours	Open All Hours	Waiting For God	The Funeral Cheering Tom Up
Red Dwarf	Red Dwarf I (Volume 1)—The End (Volume 2)—Confidence and Paranoia Red Dwarf II (Volume 1)—Kryten (Volume 2)—Stasis Leak Red Dwarf III (Volume 1)—Backwards (Volume 2)—Time Slides Red Dwarf IV Byte 1—Camille Byte 2—Dimension Jump Red Dwarf V (Volume 1)—Back to Reality (Volume 2)—Quarantine	Yes, Minister	Open Government The Writing on the Wall
		Yes, Prime Minister	The Bishop's Gambit Official Secrets The Grand Design The Key Power to the People
		The Young Ones	Volume 1 Volume 2 Volume 3 Volume 4

BIBLIOGRAPHY

AUTHOR INTERVIEWS:

George Layton - July 1995
David Croft - August 1995
Andrew Norriss - September 1995
Roy Clarke - October 1995
Peter Spence - October 1995
David Renwick - November 1995
Gorden Kaye - November 1995
Harold Snoad - January 1996
Michael Aitkens - February 1996
Susan Belbin - February 1996
Julia St. John - March 1996
Gareth Gwenlan - April 1996
Peter Bowles - May 1996
John Lloyd - June 1996
Eric Chappell - June 1996
Peter Tilbury - May 1998
Richard Briers - October 1998
Maurice Gran - December 1998
Ed Bye - March 1999
Paul Mayhew-Archer - April 1999

BOOKS:

Briers, Richard. *Natter, Natter*. London: JM Dent and Sons Ltd., 1981.

French, Dawn and Jennifer Saunders. *A Feast of French and Saunders*. London: William Heineman Ltd., 1991.

Hayward, Anthony. *Who's Who on Television*. London: Boxtree/TV Times, 1996.

Horner, Rosalie. *Inside BBC Television*. Exeter, UK: Webb and Bower Ltd., 1983.

Johnson, Kim. *The First 200 Years of Monty Python*. New York: St. Martin's Press, 1989.

Lewis, Jon E., and Penny Stempel. *Cult TV*. UK: Pavilion Books Ltd., 1993.

Lynn, Jonathan and Antony Jay. *The Complete Yes, Minister*. London: BBC Books, 1981.

Lynn, Jonathan and Antony Jay. *The Complete Yes, Prime Minister*. London: BBC Books, 1986.

Rigelsford, Adrian, Anthony Brown, and Geoff Tibballs. *Are You Being Served?*. San Francisco: KQED Books, 1995.

Taylor, Rod. *The Guinness Book of Sitcoms*. Middlesex, UK: Guinness Publishing, 1994.

Yahimagi, Tise. *British Television: an illustrated guide*. Oxford, UK: Oxford University Press, 1994.

MAGAZINE AND NEWSPAPER ARTICLES:

Busfield, Steve, and Rick Hewett. "Back in Business," *Daily Mail*, August 9, 1997.

Dutton, Julian. "All By Myself," London *Sunday Times*, May 5, 1996.

Edwards, Mark. "The Grin Reality," London *Sunday Times*, May 21, 1995.

Green, Benny. *Dad's Army* review, *Punch*, November, 1977.

Hall, John S. "Television's Funniest Man," *British Heritage*, Aug/Sept 1994.

Heald, Tim. "The Luck of The Insecure Actor," *The Radio Times*, Oct. 20–26, 1984.

Kellerman, Vivien. "Queen of British Comedy," *American Way*, August 1, 1987.

Killick, Jane. "Red Dwarf" Special Section, *Starburst*, February, 1997.

Rother, Larry. "Sitcoms with Not Much in Common," *The New York Times*, Oct. 31, 1990.

Roush, Matt. "Having Wickedly 'Fabulous' Fun," *USA Today*, July 21, 1994.

Whitney, Craig R. "Hit Show in London Dares to Spoof the French Resistance," *The New York Times*, April 26, 1988.

TV Guide, "Britain's New Fab Two," July 23, 1994.

The Box, British television magazine, June/July 1997, various articles.

Cult TV, British television magazine, various issues.

Radio Times, British television magazine, various issues.

TV Times, British television magazine, various issues.

Miscellaneous press releases and sales/promotional brochures printed and distributed by the BBC Press and Publicity Department.

INDEX

Page numbers in *italics* represent photographs.